Curs'd Example

Curs'd Example
The Duchess of Malfi and
Commonweal Tragedy

Joyce E. Peterson

University of Missouri Press
Columbia & London, 1978

Copyright © 1978 by The Curators of the University of Missouri
University of Missouri Press, Columbia, Missouri 65201
Library of Congress Catalog Card Number 77-14669
Printed and bound in the United States of America

Library of Congress Cataloging in Publication Data

Peterson, Joyce E., 1934–
  Curs'd Example.

  Bibliography: p. 115
  1. Webster, John, 1580?–1625? The Duchess of
Malfi. I. Title.
PR3184.D83P4   822'.3   77-14669
ISBN 0-8262-0240-3

For Kris, Val, and Eric—
my wise and wonderful children

Preface

My association with the Duchess began many years ago when, as an undergraduate, I was asked to appreciate and to justify my appreciation of, "I am Duchess of Malfi still." I soon realized that while I did appreciate the line, it was apparently for the wrong reasons. The context in which the Duchess speaks her line and the action leading up to it made me hear the utterance as a manifestation of John Webster's deep irony rather than of his supreme admiration for that lady. Faced with evidence that I was, thus, seriously out of step with most readers of *The Duchess of Malfi*, I decided to see, someday, if I could justify critically my impression that Webster's attitude toward his heroine was not as totally approving as virtually all the critics had assumed. The result is the present study.

On the surface, my undertaking may not seem very radical. Yet, even though there has been some modulation in recent years of critical admiration for the Duchess, most critics still apologize for suggestions that her actions characterize something other than a saint, that as *dramatic creation* she is rendered more complex and more interesting by hints of culpability. Witness Robert F. Whitman in his recent essay on "The Moral Paradox of Webster's Tragedy" (p. 897):

> As Antonio reminds us in his opening speech, princes ideally have a unique obligation to stand, in their self control, as a kind of exemplar to their people. And while it might be farfetched to associate the Duchess, rather than Ferdinand, with the "curs'd example" that spreads through "the whole land" (I.i.14–15), it seems mere romantic infatuation with her acknowledged charms to free her of substantial responsibility for what happens, or to claim her as a model of "goodness."
>
> This is, I am well aware, treading on dangerous ground, for the Duchess has earned herself a host of admirers, and I hasten to point out that I am not speaking of the woman who faces death with quiet dignity in Act IV, but of the impetuous and passionate woman of Acts I and II.

When even so tempered a suggestion of the Duchess's culpability must be followed with such careful qualification, the ground must be dangerous indeed. But exactly there I have chosen to tread.

In fairness to myself, perhaps *chosen* is not the best word. *Forced* may be more appropriate because I see the rhetorical structure of the play itself insisting on the Duchess's responsibility not only for her own fate but for the entire catastrophe as well. If to associate the Duchess with the "curs'd example" that spreads poison throughout the land—and the play—be farfetched, then it seems to me that Webster has written a melodrama not a tragedy and that those who have attacked, or apologized for, its broken-backed structure are justified. Early in the play, the Duchess assures Antonio that by accepting her proposal of marriage he will receive his overdue "wages" from Virtue for long unrewarded service. If what follows from his acceptance is intended to represent the reward for virtue, then the play does lack a consistent ethical or moral perspective, as so many have claimed.

I don't believe these charges are valid, and my purpose in this book is to establish that the play's rhetorical perspective on the Duchess informs a sound but exceedingly complex dramatic structure. Along the way, I have also attempted to delineate the generic expectations, the dramatic traditions, the historical concerns, and the topical interests constitutive of the context in which Webster was writing and his audience viewing the play. To do so seemed absolutely essential because Webster's elliptic use of generic conventions and assumption of historical and topical issues have been partially responsible for obscuring the play's perspective, especially for modern readers.

The response of Webster's audience to *The Duchess of Malfi* would, I believe, have been controlled initially by their familiarity with the sub-genre of tragedy to which it belongs, and which, for descriptive purposes, I have called "commonweal tragedy." I think, too, that the striking similarities between the actions and fate of the Duchess and Mary Queen of Scots would have had some bearing on Jacobean attitudes to Webster's heroine. In order to validate the relationship between context and perspective, I have devoted Chapters 1 and 2 to discussions of the play's critical history and total context, respectively. Building on that foundation, in the remaining chapters, I have tried to show how the play's own structure reveals Webster's judgment upon characters and action.

If my very intention seems ungallant to the Duchess's "host

of admirers," I can only ask that the questions I raise be considered. For if I have not answered them convincingly, then how much more justified may that admiration be for having been tested against those questions.

To my colleagues George Guffey and Richard Lehan, who were generous enough to read my manuscript and offer advice and encouragement, I am more grateful than I can express. The debt of gratitude I owe to Edgar Schell of the University of California, Irvine, would be embarrassing to calculate and certainly impossible to repay. Over the years, he has been teacher, adviser, critic, and friend, and there is little chance that I would have continued to pursue the study of literature or written this book were it not for my original good fortune in becoming his student. I would also like to thank Barbara Dilworth and Gary Bjork, my longtime friends, for readings and constructive suggestions. The latter especially was a prodigy of gallantry, patience, and good nature in typing through draft after draft and continuing to believe I would ever finish.

I appreciate deeply the help given me by a sabbatical leave from the University of California, Los Angeles, which enabled me to complete the penultimate version of the manuscript. And to the staff of the University of Missouri Press, my thanks for their consideration and assistance in seeing me through the final one.

J. E. P.
Los Angeles, California
October 1977

Contents

1

The Critical Dilemma

Over the years, critics have put forth so many contradictory interpretations of John Webster's meaning and intentions and such divergent estimates of his success in achieving his ends in *The Duchess of Malfi* as to suggest there is something about this play that precludes valid interpretation. This "something" might be what the play's detractors have always claimed—that it is simply a badly constructed, rhetorically uneven, sensational pastiche of Jacobean dramatic conventions and borrowed lines. On the other hand, if the play is not to be faulted, we might conclude that the critics are to be, or that there is no such thing as "valid" interpretation, or that contradictory interpretations may be equally valid. Considering how much knowledge, critical acumen, intelligence, and sensitivity most of the critics have brought to the play, I don't believe the first alternative is viable. However, neither do I believe in the impossibility of arriving at a valid interpretation nor in a critical relativism that renders all interpretations, no matter how contradictory, equally acceptable.

I would seem, then, to have come full circle, to have returned to the possibility that the play (thus, of course, the playwright) is responsible for critical disagreement over its meaning and literary value. And that, I think, is precisely where the problem does lie, but not because the play is badly flawed. On the contrary, Webster's dramatic structure is both sound and intricate, and this intricacy has invited a variety of misreadings. To my mind the most consistent misreading is of Webster's treatment of the Duchess. Considerable time spent with *The Duchess of Malfi* and its critics has led me to the conclusion that the playwright's attitude toward his heroine is the riddle to be solved if we are ever to arrive at an interpretation that takes into account the most significant number of elements in the play.

In keeping with a strong, general trend in twentieth-century criticism, much has been made in the last two decades of Webster's "ambiguities" and his "ambivalence" toward his characters, including the Duchess. Webster's attitude toward the Duchess may, I think, be described as ambivalent but not in that comfortable modern sense that allows us to dismiss as gestures-toward-orthodoxy the philosophical, religious, or political values informing works of times and places not our own. Twentieth-century discomfort with the orthodoxy of our great authors is evidenced, for example, by all the criticism that assumes Chaucer's ambivalence about "medieval" Christianity or Shakespeare's about the doctrine of order and degree. Apparently, it is not only comforting to believe that they shared our own uncertainties, but that these uncertainties are, somehow, the very mark of their greatness.

Not that I would deny Chaucer, Shakespeare, or Webster his dark nights of the uncertain soul. On the contrary, I suspect that Keats was right in implying that the capacity for having such nights is constitutive of genius, but it is the capacity for transcending those dark nights, at least aesthetically, which is definitive of the literature we call great. I believe, somewhat unfashionably I suppose, that in Webster's case this transcendence is enabled by a commitment, in the play, to certain values that also dictate his attitude toward the Duchess. His "ambivalence" consists in his capacity for judging her on more than one basis and allowing the play's rhetoric to imply which of these bases has greater communal value. The complexity of this rhetoric creates the major stumbling block to interpretations of the play.

Paradoxically, the very felicity of Webster's dramatic creation of the Duchess is the most immediate source of difficulty. There are those women in literature, as there are in history, who so dominate the spheres in which they move, so engage our sympathies, and so charm our imaginations that they reduce all questions of ethical or moral standards to niggling. To judge them seems, at best, insensitivity, at worst, a priggish moralism. Webster's Duchess is such a woman. Critical history of the play attests to her power to forestall judgment or, more precisely, to forestall our recognition of the play's judgment upon her. Until fairly recently, admiration—indeed, adulation—of the Duchess was practically universal, and I believe that admiration for her as dramatic creation, as element in the larger structure of *The Duchess of Malfi*, is richly justified. Unfortunately, the admiration afforded her has generally overstepped the boundaries of the play. Criticism seems to have granted her an extra-dramatic existence. Critics have repeatedly discussed Webster's Duchess as though she were a historic personage to whom and for whom the events at Malfi, Rome, and Ancona were unlucky historical accidents, not carefully plotted incidents in Webster's dramatic action.[1]

This tendency is made obvious in the ubiquity of quotation and response to her most famous line, "I am Duchess of Malfi still." At some point or other in study after study of Renaissance literature or intellectual history, it is bound to be quoted. Works not primarily about *The Duchess* usually present the line as illustrative of that dark moment when disillusioned Renaissance humanism recognized that the certainty of cosmic order was gone and that man must find and reestablish through his individual identity the meaning lost along with that certainty. If the study is primarily concerned with Webster's work, the line is most often quoted in lyric culmination of a defense of the Duchess as redeeming spirit of the play—if not of the world itself. Critic after critic has capped his panegyric of the Duchess by quoting this line as the ultimate expression of her self-affirmation, exultant humanity, Christian Stoicism, integrity of life, and/or triumphant individualism in the face of the inherent meaninglessness and evil of her world—and, by extension, our own.[2]

Unfortunately, the more the Duchess comes to be regarded as the redeeming spirit of the play, the more it must be regarded as a play that sorely needs redeeming. For if Webster intended us to see the Duchess solely as a charming, somewhat frail, but ultimately innocent and transcending individualist trapped in a decadent and evil society, there is much in the play that is undeniably ambiguous, obscure, or inconsistent—if not flatly contradictory.

The questions have been asked repeatedly by the play's detractors: Why does Webster set up the norm for princely behavior in Antonio's opening speech and then fail to apply it? If the Duchess is both innocent and virtuous, why does Webster expose her to the excess of cruelty in Act 4? Given his approval of her relationship with Antonio, why does Webster parody her behavior in Julia's secret liaison with the Cardinal and brazen wooing of Bosola? If the Duchess's suffering and redemption

1. Of course, she is a historical personage. Nevertheless, we obviously can't ignore Aristotle's distinction between history and poetry.

2. To list all the critics who have done so would be tedious and fruitless. A typical example is: "The Duchess shows us not what we are, but what it is possible for us to become; she vindicates the tragic dignity of the human spirit." James P. Driscoll, "Integrity of Life in *The Duchess of Malfi,*" p. 50.

are his central concerns, why does the play continue after her death into the grotesqueries of Act 5? These questions are not the only ones that have been or might be asked, but they do point to the two charges that have consistently informed attacks on and defenses of the play throughout its critical history, the charges that it is structurally incoherent and rhetorically inconsistent.

Since few critics would fault the Duchess, the old lines of criticism were drawn on either side of these issues, with the Duchess cited as an exception to the play's general weakness or superlative expression of its virtues. In protesting too much, the play's defenders have often revealed that they do not see any readily identifiable structural principle or rhetorical perspective informing its action. They have argued for imagistic and atmospheric unity as saving cohesive principles in the play. Some have retreated implicitly or explicitly to an acceptance of imitative form to explain the apparently chance relationship of some of its incidents and the lack of informing values.[3] Many, following Rupert Brooke's lead, have rejected the importance of plot when it is balanced against the play's affective power.[4]

More recently, the lines have been redrawn with the question of values or anti-values taking precedence. There is an assumption on all sides that the play is not structurally flawed but rather informed by a perspective that the other sides have failed to see. There are, on the far left, mutatis mutandis, the descendants of those who argued from imitative form. They see Webster as an Ur-existentialist who makes a dramatic virtue of the meaninglessness of his world. The play's very lack of coherence attests and gives anti-form to his perspective: The brilliance of verisimilitude "is the emotional result of a lack of any integrating philosophy on Webster's part. He hammers his plays together with a violence of will."[5] Under this rubric, "those critics

3. See, for example, Hereward T. Price, "The Function of Imagery in Webster," on imagistic unity; M. C. Bradbrook, "Fate and Chance in *The Duchess of Malfi,*" from "Two Notes Upon Webster," on imitative form (implicitly). The most recent statement that argues for the play's structural coherence as its imitation of an incoherent world is this: "Somehow it is necessary to make clear that uncertainty and confusion are not flaws in the construction of the play, but its very essence," Lois Potter, "Realism Versus Nightmare: Problems of Staging *The Duchess of Malfi,*" in *The Triple Bond: Plays, Mainly Shakespearean, in Performance,* ed. Joseph G. Price, p. 182.

4. Rupert Brooke, *John Webster and The Elizabethan Drama,* p. 123.

5. Richard A. Bodtke, *Tragedy and the Jacobean Temper: The Major Plays of John Webster,* ed. James Hogg, p. 90.

who resolve to wrest clear-cut convictions from his works reduce them to mere statements of despair."[6]

Moving very slightly to the right, we find those who identify Webster as Stoic (sometimes Christian Stoic). Within this camp, few would accept that Jacobean playwrights such as Webster could give credence "to that hotch-potch of antiquated science, fancy, and folklore dignified by some modern scholars as the Elizabethan World Order."[7] For these critics the play's virtue is its realization through characters and their actions of the Stoic sense that value and meaning depend on the individual's ability to rise above a corrupt and corrupting society by living according to his own principles, regardless of consequence.

There are, as I said, some Christian Stoics in this camp, but generally the Christian apologists for the play are to be found on the far right. For them, the play is rigorously informed by a basically medieval Christian theology, and Webster intends to demonstrate the ways in which God moves mysteriously in the affairs of men. One critic goes so far as to call *The Duchess of Malfi* a theodicy.[8] Obviously, such readings find an absolute standard in the play for judging its actions and characters. No questions of ambivalence or ambiguity here. One might anticipate, given such a standard, that the attitude toward the Duchess would be consistent, but that is not the case.

Interestingly, just as the earlier critics generally agreed on the Duchess's virtue, regardless of their critical stances, within almost all of these later factions, some have reservations about Webster's unqualified approval of her. This may, perhaps, bear out Clifford Leech's contention that "the more we consider the Duchess the more hints of guilt seem to appear."[9] Leech was the first critic to suggest and consistently pursue the question of the Duchess's responsibility for the events in the play leading to her own death and the catastrophes of Act 5. The basis of his judgment is largely political: The Duchess is culpable because she does not behave responsibly *as a duchess.* This political emphasis characterizes a rather small faction, somewhat to the right of center since it does assume Webster's political orthodoxy.

6. David Cook, "The Extreme Situation: A Study of Webster's Tragedies," p. 9.

7. John W. Lever, *The Tragedy of State,* p. 5.

8. D. C. Gunby, *"The Duchess of Malfi:* A Theological Approach," in *John Webster: Proceedings of the York Symposium,* ed. Brian Morris, p. 181.

9. Clifford Leech, *John Webster: A Critical Study,* p. 75.

As my reading of the play will illustrate, I believe a political approach the most fruitful because it renders coherent a larger number of elements than any of the other approaches I have been discussing. Among critics who assume that Webster's perspective is orthodox, those such as Leech, J. L. Calderwood, and Fernand Lagarde who discuss the Duchess's actions in political terms have produced more balanced readings than those such as Eloise Goreau who have examined her moral probity under the standard of Christian theology. While the former are able to weigh her virtues against her political failings, or those of her brothers, the latter, generally, are committed to seeing her as totally unregenerate or as a sort of Christian martyr, which does rather coincide with her own implied attitude immediately preceding her death.

The most obvious consequence of fully Christian readings of the play, whether they canonize or anathematize the Duchess, is their tendency to reduce the play to a kind of tract, very much in the *Mirror for Magistrates* tradition. Actually, Goreau readily admits that her Christian, allegorical reading transforms the play into a morality drama.[10] It is, however, thoroughgoing in its condemnation of the Duchess and, thus far, one of the only two commentaries that do not evidence a certain reluctance—if not uneasiness—in treating her ungallantly.[11] So, for the most part, the Duchess retains her critical immunity, standing somehow above the summary judgment that interpretations of the play's evaluative perspective would seem to dictate.

In trying to come to terms with this phenomenon, much can be said for Dover Wilson's approach in *The Fortunes of Falstaff* (Cambridge, England, 1961). Since Wilson was prompted by a sense that Falstaff had "escaped" from the *Henry IV* plays, that a critical myth of Falstaff had taken over and clouded interpretations of those plays, and that as Falstaff's fortune had risen, the plays' had declined, the analogies between his critical problems and mine are obvious. Despite the obvious excess into which Wilson's methodology leads him of punishing Falstaff

10. Eloise K. Goreau, *Integrity of Life: Allegorical Imagery in the Plays of John Webster,* ed. James Hogg, p. 164.

11. The other scholar who finds virtually total condemnation of the Duchess in the play is Muriel West, *The Devil and John Webster,* ed. James Hogg. West does, as her editors feared in the "Foreword" of this work, tend to "overplay her cards" in this study of demonology and witchcraft, as they are invoked by the imagery of Webster's major tragedies. However, she does offer some intriguing ideas and information and some provocative insights in locating the presence of devils in *The Duchess.*

for the sins of critics, the thoroughness with which he eluci-
dates the relationship between the morality tradition and
Shakespeare's dramatic structure in 1 and 2 *Henry IV* should
leave little doubt about the rhetorical perspective implied by
that structure on Falstaff. Yet enough doubt obviously does
remain to indicate that we cannot assume that simply by recon-
stituting the habits of mind, the world picture, the values, and
the dramatic tradition that, say, Samuel Johnson shared with
Shakespeare but we have lost, we will arrive at definitive clarification of the play's rhetorical perspective.[12]

Certainly, a great deal has been done to re-create the context
of Renaissance England in which plays such as *Henry IV* were
written. There has been abundant reconstruction of the native
and classical conventions informing Renaissance drama, of the
religious, philosophical, historical, and political habits of the
"Renaissance Mind," and of the public opinion, topical concerns, even gossip, of the Elizabethan and Jacobean periods.[13]
All of this has been invaluable in enabling us to hypothesize
about the ways in which a Renaissance playwright might expect his audience to react to allusions, characters, and situations. Yet, despite these reconstructions and Wilson's admirable
effort, the controversy over how Shakespeare expected his audience to react to Falstaff rages on. Nor have explications of the
Renaissance attitude toward the remarriage of widows, for example, brought about any agreement over Webster's attitude
toward the Duchess's second marriage.

That these and other venerable problems of Renaissance literature have refused to yield their solutions to such reconstructions of context made a recent comment of Wayne C. Booth's
especially provocative for me:

> No matter how much biographical or historical information we
> need or use in making our reconstructions, they are finally built
> into patterns of shared literary expectations—the grooves of
> genre, the trajectories of aroused expectations and gratifica-
> tions.[14]

Generic expectations are, after all, part of the context in which
a play is written. If we are going to bring context to bear in
interpreting a play, we must take those expectations into ac-

12. J. Dover Wilson, *The Fortunes of Falstaff*, p. 7.
13. I have in mind the work of such as Farnham, Baker, Owst, Bevington,
Spivack, Tillyard, Rossiter, G. B. Harrison; see bibliography.
14. Wayne C. Booth, *A Rhetoric of Irony*, p. 100.

count or the context will be incomplete. More important, we must identify and assume appropriate generic expectations or the context will be inexact. Faced with the proliferation of verdicts based on the same sets of evidence about *The Duchess,* it occurred to me that, perhaps, the expectations about genre that we have brought to the play are not the appropriate ones.

I have, of course, been partially anticipated here by a number of recent studies of Webster's work. Given the tremendous interest in genre stimulated by E. D. Hirsch's *Validity in Interpretation,* it is predictable that this critical tack should show itself in a group of studies that attempt, primarily or incidentally, to redefine the genre of *The Duchess of Malfi* and, thus, to readjust the implications, emphases, and values of the play. Unfortunately, disagreements about what genre Webster did intend and, thus, what sorts of implications can legitimately be drawn from the play have resulted in as much confusion as that generated by the other critical approaches. The multiplicity of genres identified and the assurance with which judgments are made on the bases of those genres seem to bear out Hirsch's suggestion that "an interpreter's preliminary generic conception of a text is constitutive of everything that he subsequently understands and . . . this remains the case unless and until that generic conception is altered."[15]

It is hard to imagine a critical relativism that could accept as equally valid the numerous contradictory claims about and based upon genre. For one critic, the genre of *The Duchess* is comi-tragedy, for another tragicomedy. Although which element takes precedence is at issue between them, both would agree that the genre, in part, implies that the play is "written in the service of no identifiable absolute, whether political, moral, or religious."[16] Webster's purpose is to contemplate man's rootlessness and uncertainty or to make us satirically muse at them.[17] Obviously, this judgment brings these critics into conflict with Goreau for whom the play is a Christian tragedy informed by a theology in which the prince must function as Christian exemplar for his people. She focuses on the theological rather than the political aspect of this exemplary

15. E. D. Hirsch, Jr., *Validity in Interpretation,* p. 74.

16. J. R. Mulryne, "Webster and the Uses of Tragicomedy," in *John Webster: Proceedings of the York Symposium,* ed. Brian Morris, pp. 137–38.

17. Normand Berlin, *"The Duchess of Malfi:* Act V and Genre," p. 360.

role: "As nature mirrors God's order in the macrocosm, so the king should mirror God; and the subjects should look into the mirror of the king to find their own example."[18]

Insistence on the play's religious aspect puts her at odds with those for whom its genre is political in emphasis. For one political interpreter the play is a tragedy of State, but the State is the villain; revenge is one of the individual's legitimate options in the face of its power to corrupt; and the reply "I am Duchess of Malfi still" is "an affirmation of reason and an assertion of the Stoic kingship of the mind, undismayed by tyranny."[19] This accords ill with Lagarde's identification of the play as a Machiavellian tragedy in which the grasping self-interest of individuals is responsible for corruption of the State and "I am Duchess of Malfi still" is an ironic condemnation of the Duchess's failure to act as ruler and prevent that corruption.

Focusing on the revenge element in the play, several critics have ignored Brooke's dismissal of revenge as other than efficient cause and claimed that its presence in the play is generically definitive. For one, the revenge mode undercuts what is implicitly a romantic tragedy and presents the Duchess's and Antonio's love as paradoxically not only self-fulfillment but also horror, decay, and punishment.[20] For another, the reversal of the generic expectations that the protagonist of revenge tragedy should be a man "forces us into a real awareness of the dissonances of Webster's world."[21] This position is undercut by another critic's claim that, as a matter of fact, men *are* the protagonists of the play, Ferdinand and the Cardinal, and Bosola's revenge on them serves as a powerful redemptive force.[22] This generic reading certainly sidesteps the problem of the play's perspective on the Duchess because she retains neither her role as heroine nor as redeeming spirit of the play.

Despite the contradictions and distortions of the play's structure and rhetoric in this category of criticism, I believe that Hirsch is correct in maintaining that "valid interpretation is always governed by a valid inference about genre"[23] and that

18. Goreau, *Integrity of Life*, p. 100.

19. Lever, *The Tragedy of State*, p. 94.

20. Charles R. Forker, "Love, Death, and Fame: The Grotesque Tragedy of John Webster."

21. Bodtke, *Tragedy and the Jacobean Temper*, pp. 214–15. I will discuss this question more fully in Chapter 2.

22. Melvin Seiden, *The Revenge Tragedy in Websterian Tragedy*, ed. James Hogg.

23. Hirsch, *Validity in Interpretation*, p. 113.

the risk of being caught (and caught out) in a hermeneutical circle is worth taking. It is especially worth taking in behalf of *The Duchess* because the play itself furnishes so much evidence that Webster expected generic features to carry considerable formal and rhetorical weight. The juxtaposition of scenes and metaphors and the extremely elliptic use of conventional features create a kind of rhetorical shorthand. Since Webster's fastidious care with his work is legendary, his reliance on the rhetorical force of this shorthand implies how confident he was that the system of conventions that constitutes the genre would be recognized by his audience and could, thus, be counted on to convey the implications he intended.

By their very nature, of course, genres imply limitations of meaning and possibilities of response. To take a broad and simplistic example, because of our literary experience, we do not expect choices to be revocable in tragedy nor characters to be deeply sympathetic in comedy; and we speak of tragic vision and comic vision, assuming that they are mutually exclusive in their purest form. The evolution of new and sub-genres is impelled by and expressive of refinements of such visions, of more complex, more specifically defined perspectives on experience as it is represented in literary form. As a genre matures, we say it becomes more conventional and thus more immediately identifiable. And this process is indicative of two phenomena: First, that poets and playwrights have recognized that certain rhetorical and formal elements of a genre invoke, more efficiently and effectively than others, the perspective on experience that characterizes the genre and, in a given work, most nearly coincides with their own perspective; second, that readers and audiences share that recognition. Thus, the conventions of a genre serve both to identify it and to imply its perspective on the world, that is, its informing principles of value.[24]

In her study of genre theory in the Renaissance, Rosalie Colie discusses her sense that the very nature of a genre (or "kind")

24. See Hirsch, *Validity in Interpretation,* p. 93: "Because the types must be shared in order to carry implications, and because they would not be shared if the interpreter did not know the type, it is genuinely descriptive to call an intrinsic genre a system of conventions"; and p. 222: "By classifying the text as belonging to a particular genre, the interpreter automatically posits a general horizon for its meaning. The genre provides a sense of the whole, a notion of typical meaning components."

can be trusted to invoke this perspective (or "set") and to establish a general boundary of meaning for a literary work:

> I am trying to express something of the *social force and function of the kinds, as abbreviations for a "set" on the world,* as definitions of manageable boundaries, some large, some small, in which material can be treated and considered. *Social too in the sense that, these sets and boundaries understood, a great deal need not be said about them: One needn't recapitulate all pastoral values in a dialogue set in Urbino the well-named, when one can show by various signposts that pastoral values are understood as part of this work's urbanity* [my emphases]. Since whatever generic definitions a writer or culture espouses, examples willy-nilly accumulate in generic categories, the kinds can easily be seen acting as tiny subcultures with their own habits, habitats, and structures of ideas as well as their own forms.[25]

Webster constructed a number of the signposts Colie speaks of, conventional features that clearly establish his set on the world of the play and reveal the habits, habitats, and structures of ideas of his generic "subculture." Critical disagreement over Webster's set, especially his evaluative perspective on the Duchess results not from his ambiguity, his failure to erect clear signposts to his intended end, but from our failure to read those generic signposts as such.

Ironically, post-seventeenth-century critics appear to have been in the same situation vis à vis *The Duchess* that Hirsch describes as the plight of *Don Juan's* first audience:

> Older genre conventions both guided Byron's invention and nourished it, but it is obvious that the genre idea of *Don Juan* is Byron's alone and is a new kind that had never existed before. One reason Byron felt obliged to lard the poem with so many explicit explanations of what he was up to was that his readers needed signposts which he did not have to provide in the somewhat more traditional genre of *Childe Harold.*[26]

Byron did not have to provide explicit signposts in *Childe Harold* because the conventional ones were there, and he could depend on his audience's familiarity with the implications of those conventions to enable them to follow his directions. Obviously, the "genre idea" of *The Duchess of Malfi* was not Webster's alone, and he could make the same assumptions about his audience's

25. Rosalie Colie, *The Resources of Kind: Genre Theory in the Renaissance,* pp. 115–16.
26. Hirsch, *Validity in Interpretation,* p. 106.

needs that Byron could make about those of readers of *Childe Harold*. But it is equally obvious from post-Restoration criticism of the play that these same assumptions can no longer be made. The widely divergent implications drawn by critics from the play seem to bear out the truth of another of Hirsch's contentions:

> Implications are derived from a shared type that has been learned, and, therefore, *the generation of implications depends on the interpreter's previous experience of the shared type.* The principle for generating implications is, ultimately and in the broadest sense, a learned convention.[27]

Paradoxically, the interpreters' previous experience of the conventions used by Webster has often resulted in their being dismissed as merely conventional. Why does Webster include Antonio's opening speech on the "fix'd order" of government? What is the purpose of the subplot involving Julia? What is the logic of Webster's *sententiae?* How can Ferdinand's fable of Reputation be justified? What is the function of the Pilgrims in Act 3? Why does Webster bring in the madmen in Act 4? What are we to make of the contrived "coincidences" of Act 5? Each of these questions has been answered with "convention"—dramatic, political, or social. Certainly not all critics have responded thus, but their number is sufficient to imply that we no longer consider these conventions viable and constitutive elements of the play's meaning. Rather, as a recent BBC production of *The Duchess of Malfi* evidenced in its cutting of many of these and other conventions, we seem to consider them traditional excrescences, sops to orthodoxy, or comfortable handholds for the Renaissance audience.

In fairness to modern producers, however, I must admit that there might be justification for expecting some hardening of the conventional arteries in *The Duchess.* I agree with Ralph Berry's comment that, formally, the play was "distinctly old fashioned at the time of its appearance."[28] In a decade when most playwrights had turned to tragic genres concerned with the plight of the individual, with Stoicism, with Machiavellianism, with revenge, Webster anachronistically, but effectively, returned to a genre that Shakespeare, for example, had dignified considerably up to and including his production of *King Lear* and *Macbeth.*

27. Ibid., p. 66.
28. Ralph Berry, *The Art of John Webster,* p. 6.

In the next half dozen years, however, it became rather passé, and one might expect the playwright either to parody or attempt to avoid the conventions that would obviously date it.

Webster did neither. He did not have to because the second decade of the seventeenth century provided a context that gave the somewhat old-fashioned genre of *The Duchess of Malfi* tremendously viable ironic significance. For Webster's Jacobean audience, the genre's conventions pointed, of course, to the ideals—political, historical, and dramatic—which were part of its set on the world. They could not have avoided seeing how those conventions thus underlined, ironically and satirically, the disparity between ideal and "actuality" in the world of the play—especially since it mirrored so relentlessly that same disparity in their own world.[29] Rarely have political ideals and political realities drifted further apart than they did in the court of King James I.

This ironic tension between generic ideals and political actuality informs the rhetorical perspective that gives structural coherence to *The Duchess of Malfi*. To understand that rhetorical perspective and its implicit judgment on the Duchess, it is necessary to examine the nature of the genre and the way in which historical event, political theory, dramatic tradition, and topical concern came together to create the context that gave it ironic significance. These are the concerns of my next chapter.

29. See the introduction by John Russell Brown in his edition of *The Duchess of Malfi,* pp. xxxviii–xli, particularly, for a discussion of "Webster's England" and its bearing on the play.

2

The Conscience of the King

A fearful concern about the tension between ideals of order and the potentially anarchic individual will is certainly as old as any form of human government. Yet, in looking at the historical-political context in which Webster wrote *The Duchess of Malfi,* it is clear that for Jacobeans, particularly, the last two hundred years or so of English history had been marked by events that might transform that concern into obsession. From the time of Richard II's downfall, the country had been continually shaken with political troubles generated by the will of its sovereigns, or of those plotting or battling against them.

Richard's rise-and-fall was essentially a *psychomachia* in which the "king's two bodies" were at war. The will of the "body natural" so fought against the responsibilities of the "body politic" that Richard could not maintain the precarious balance between the two within his person as king.[1] To put it in less medieval, philosophical terms, Richard repeatedly placed his private desires and his personal will above his public responsibilities and the weal of his subjects. He lavished attention, wealth, and power on his favorites and pursued domestic and foreign policies dictated by their advice and his personal priorities. Thus, he burdened his subjects with unfair laws and excessive taxation, blackened his reputation as king, and lost the respect, love, and loyalty of his subjects, thereby creating the conditions for his deposition and the accession of Bolingbroke in 1399.[2]

The seeds of dissension sown in that action flowered in the Wars of the Roses, which virtually encompassed the century that followed. In that long bloody struggle for the crown, most of the contenders showed themselves more desirous of personal power, glory, and privilege than of establishing and maintain-

1. For a literary discussion of this see Maynard Mack, *Killing the King: Three Studies in Shakespeare's Tragic Structure,* pp. 3–10. Mack's understanding and explication of this concept of kingship is based largely upon Ernest Kantorowicz's *The King's Two Bodies.* Kantorowicz's book contains a fine chapter on *Richard II.*
2. See May MacKisack, *The Fourteenth Century: 1307–1399,* particularly Chapter 15.

14

ing order for the commonweal. To be sure, at the struggle's end, Henry VII seemed to aim at such order when he established absolute monarchy and reduced the nobility's power. But despite the whitewashing of Tudor propagandists, these moves probably had more to do with his own dour, pecunious temperament and dynastic ambitions than with a commitment to his larger public responsibility as sovereign.

His son's temperament may have been vastly different, but in his desire for absolute power and the perpetuation of the Tudor dynasty, Henry VIII showed a will as radical as his father's, a will without respect for the individual consciences of his subjects. On the one hand, Henry strengthened the monarchy and, thus, its potential for maintaining order: By placing his dynastic concerns above the prerogatives of the Papacy, he could claim his divine right to the throne directly from God—without any intermediation of the Church. On the other hand, as the religio-political wranglings that convulsed the nation during the reigns of his children testify, by identifying the sovereign's will with the will of God and making obedience to him a sacred duty, the "Tudor Myth" made dissent not only treasonous, but potentially heretical. Such a political theology dictated that political battles would be fought as holy wars and also collapsed political ethics into morality. In the name of humane consistency, it followed that the prince certainly should evidence, or be discreet enough to claim, absolute moral probity as exemplary proof of his divine sanction. Since the people were completely at his mercy and owed him obedience despite his character, they could only regard him as a scourge for their own sinfulness should he be wicked.[3]

His exemplary role had another dimension: It served not simply as an indication of divine sanction but as a normative model for the people's own behavior. His responsibility as exemplar for the moral health of the nation is a recurrent theme of the political writings aimed at the education of princes. Sir Thomas Elyot, for instance, recommends that these verses of Claudian be graven on a tablet and placed in the ruler's bedchamber:

3. See M. M. Reese, *The Tudors and Stuarts,* for a concise, comprehensive discussion of the establishment and development of the Tudor dynasty and myth and Chapter 10, particularly, for a discussion of the question of Divine Right. See also, Lewis Einstein, *Tudor Ideals,* Part 1, for further clarification of the ideals I've been discussing.

Be nat moche meued with singular appetite
Except it profite unto thy subiectes all.
At thyne example the people wyll delite
Be it vice or vertue, with the[e] they rise or fall.
No laues auaile, men tourne as doth a ball
For where the ruler in liuynge is not stable
Bothe laue and counsaile is tourned into a fable.[4]

Predictably, these didactic works also repeatedly emphasize that a prince must avoid occasions of temptation. One sure way was to surround himself with only virtuous courtiers and counsellors. The fear that favorites or unscrupulous counsellors will influence or corrupt the prince is obviously very valid when men believe that the moral, as well as the political, health of the nation depends on his will.

If a courtier or counsellor was to be feared as capable of turning the sovereign's eye away from the common weal toward the gratification of personal appetites, how much more might the influence of a spouse be dreaded? With Mary Tudor's reign, this became an especially pertinent question. The fear that she might place her personal desires as a woman before the best interests of the nation reached its height during the negotiations for and following her marriage to Philip of Spain.[5] This fear was intensified, of course, by the religious implications of this Catholic alliance for a Protestant England, but it was also, and more basically, complicated by the traditional nature of marriage in which the wife owed obedience and subservience to the husband. In other words, her will was, theoretically, no longer her own.[6] How much worse the case might be if love or "carnal affection" should be an element in the marriage is expressed in Elyot's comment: "Wherefore Plato sayeth, that the soule of man, which is by loue possessed, dieth in his own body, and lyueth in another."[7] Obviously the balance of the "Queen's two bodies" would be radically upset.

As it turned out, the failures and excesses of Mary's reign could not be blamed on her marriage to Philip. Nevertheless, these concerns were constantly on the nation's mind during the

4. Sir Thomas Elyot, *The Book of the Governour*, p. 120.
5. See Reese, *The Tudors and Stuarts*, pp. 88–96.
6. See Carroll Camden, *The Elizabethan Woman*, p. 252ff. for a discussion of contemporary views. Also, Lewis Einstein, *Tudor Ideals*, Part 2, Chapter 5.
7. Elyot, *The Book of the Governour*, p. 250.

rule of Elizabeth. Exasperated with female rule, her subjects at first hoped she would marry; then, later, as it became clear that she really did not intend to do so, hope turned to anxiety over the succession, and they pressed her harder than ever. But as M. M. Reese remarks:

> Elizabeth knew better than her critics. Her virginity became the symbol of that national independence which it was her mission to defend. If she married a foreign Prince, she bound herself and her people to serve his interests. She might marry one of her subjects. . . . But if she married at all, she threw away her strongest weapon. The Queen of England was the best marriage in Europe: unmarried, she kept all Europe hopeful and expectant, unwilling to fight against her if they might conquer her by wooing; married, she lost her power. Early in her reign she had to master her personal feelings. . . . Whatever her private impulses were, she suppressed them in her duty to her people.[8]

History bears out Reese's judgment that Elizabeth was wiser than those who urged her to marry. She went to her grave the Virgin Queen, and whether or not this was really a matter of subordinating her private desires and personal will to the weal of her country, she was not averse to having her subjects see it that way. Finally, they may have breathed a sigh of relief that she never allowed an unwise marriage to polarize and strengthen the religio-political factions living in uneasy detente throughout her reign. They had a near and dangerous example of the consequences of such action in Mary Queen of Scots.

Living in virtual or actual imprisonment in England for almost twenty years and presented as a potential destroyer of the peace and displacer of the official Protestant faith, Mary Stuart could not have helped but become an exemplar for most Englishmen of culpable un-wisdom and anarchic will in a ruler. Her disregard of policy, her lack of discretion in choosing courtiers and counsellors, her insistence on marrying men whose primary recommendation was their personal attractiveness to her, and her willingness to compromise her reputation through ambiguous action led, it must have seemed, inexorably to her loss of crown and her imprisonment, first in Scotland and then in England. Regardless of her courage, her charm and beauty, her ready wit and resourcefulness, Mary's career was a precise

8. Reese, *The Tudors and Stuarts,* p. 104.

charting of the consequences when a ruler places her private
desires above reputation, political realities, and public responsibility and her will above the weal of her subjects.[9]

1. Political Dramaturgy and Commonweal Tragedy

Whether one accepts the classical or the native tradition as
the most immediate formal influence on Renaissance tragedy in
England, I think there can be no question that the genres of
serious English drama reflect not only the shaping influence of
these historical events but of these political concerns as well.
The history plays and tragedies repeatedly dramatize conflicts
reflective of the political philosophy that sees the sovereign as
absolute and his will and example as dictating the health or
corruption of the nation. However, I agree with such scholars
as Willard Farnham, E. M. W. Tillyard, A. P. Rossiter, David
Bevington, Irving Ribner, and Bernard Spivack that in the native tradition one form lent itself admirably to the dramatic
expression of this philosophy and of Tudor propaganda. This
form was, of course, the morality play, and the domination of
the stage by the political morality drama during the middle and
late middle years of the sixteenth century attests to its useful-
ness, and its popularity.

Exactly why it lent itself so well to these ends is explained
by Ribner:

> The morality drama contained elements admirably suited to the
> dramatic presentation of history in such a way that the didactic
> ends of Tudor historiography might be served. There was first a
> sense of form by which the elements of history could be related
> to one another and made to constitute a meaningful whole. The
> stock morality device of *Humanum Genus* torn between good and
> evil angels, for instance, could easily be translated into terms of
> a king torn between good and evil counsellors, as we have so
> clearly illustrated in *Woodstock* and *Richard II.* The dramatic pattern
> of the morality play became part of the greatest history plays of
> the age of Elizabeth, where it is perhaps most perfectly and strik-
> ingly evidenced in *Henry IV.* There were, secondly, elements of
> symbol and allegory by means of which the matter of history

9. For a discussion of public opinion of Mary Stuart in England during the
sixteenth and seventeenth centuries, see James Emerson Phillips, *Images of a
Queen: Mary Stuart in Sixteenth Century Literature.*

could be both identified with contemporary political situations and made to teach general political lessons.[10]

Bevington thoroughly examines the appeal of the form on that second count in his study of *Tudor Drama and Politics*. As he remarks of *Magnyfycence,* Skelton's choice of the morality form was dictated by an awareness that "its guidance of moral response is unambiguous and polemical."[11] In other words, the playwright could rely and capitalize on the audience's generic expectations. When a man sat down to watch a Tudor interlude, he expected to be admonished about something; he expected to see enacted, usually allegorically, "a sequential thesis in fulfillment of an instructive purpose."[12] The writers of these political dramas did their best to satisfy this expectation. From the beginning of its secularization to the eventual development of the history plays and the genre of tragedy I am attempting to define, this strain of native drama never lost is didactic thrust. Its focus may have switched from salvation of the individual to salvation of the body politic, but it never stopped pointing out the road to that salvation.

I do not believe we would need the critical statements of a Sidney or Greville in order to realize what the end and function of tragedy were for Renaissance Englishmen. The rhetorical perspectives informing the plays furnish implicit evidence that the theater continued to take seriously the function that the morality drama so overtly and explicitly proclaimed. There is a sense in these dramas, created in no small part by the very use of conventional elements taken over from the moralities, that as the ruler was to be exemplar, so the drama attempted to provide him with examples of the consequences of mis-rule and his subjects with the consequences of rebelling against his rule, regardless of its quality.

Nor was the drama of this factional era limited to admonition concerning abstract political norms. As Bevington has shown so comprehensively, playwrights other than Skelton or Sackville and Norton (in the well-known case of *Gorboduc*) directed their attention to immediate political problems and aimed their plays

10. Irving Ribner, *The English History Play in the Age of Shakespeare,* pp. 40–41.
11. David Bevington, *Tudor Drama and Politics: A Critical Approach to Topical Meaning,* p. 58.
12. Bernard Spivack, *Shakespeare and the Allegory of Evil,* p. 102.

to suggest immediate solutions. Even at the end of the Elizabethan era, as Bevington remarks of Shakespeare and Jonson, dramatists "still believed in the power of art to guide and reform. Political dramaturgy was an inescapable and major portion of their heritage."[13] That it was an inescapable and major portion of Webster's heritage is evidenced by *The Duchess of Malfi*. This heritage of political dramaturgy is part of that context that, as I claimed above, gave viable ironic significance to the genre of which the play is a late, if not the last, example.

I do not intend, here, nor would it be to the point, to trace the evolution of Webster's genre out of the morality tradition. That would require detailed analysis of the way in which inclusion of more and more particularized material in the secular and political moralities enabled, and finally forced, the shift from the allegorical to the representational mode. It would also require a lengthy discussion of the generative convulsion that resulted when the informing logic of these modes came into conflict.[14] Certainly, understanding this evolution is vital to understanding the nature of Renaissance drama generally, but my present concern is more specific. I want to examine a limited number of elements in Webster's dramatic heritage that originated in the morality drama. By doing so, I hope to establish that the very presence of these elements in a play invoked the assumptions and intentions originally informing them in the moralities and that the audience's familiarity with this significance would enable their use as rhetorically normative cues.

It is precisely because Webster could count upon these generic signposts to carry implications and imply judgments that he uses his conventions so elliptically and, for those who shared that same context, so unambiguously. For those of us who do not share this heritage so immediately, reconstruction of that aspect of Webster's context is more problematical than the sort of reconstruction of historical concerns or political theories I have just attempted. Trying to re-create intellectually the effect

13. Bevington, *Tudor Drama and Politics,* p. 4.

14. Elsewhere I have made an attempt to discuss that generative convulsion; see Joyce E. Peterson, "The Paradox of Disintegrating Form in *Mundus et Infans.*" My understanding of the morality form, its development, and its influence on Elizabethan and Jacobean drama is deeply informed by those scholars whose works are cited in the bibliography. It would be virtually impossible for me to sort out each scholar's contribution to my understanding and it would hardly be suitable repayment of that debt to engage in tedious citation at every point, could I accomplish that sorting out.

of a dramatic convention is, obviously, a far and feeble cry from immediate emotional and imaginative response to it in performance. Nevertheless, I think such a reconstruction is worth attempting: without it, Webster's perspective remains clouded.

That aspect of the morality drama most apparently adaptable to the expression of orthodox political theory was its basic formal given. In the purest form of the morality, the ground of action represents the Soul. The central character represents Will, whose choice among the alternative modes of behavior personified by the other characters dictates the condition of that ground.[15] If he follows the counsel of Conscience, Charity, or Humility, the ground of the play is a state of grace; if he capitulates to the enticements of Folly, Avarice, or Pride, the ground is a state of sin. Given the analogical habit of mind that the Renaissance inherited from the Middle Ages, this absolute affective relationship between the Will and the moral health of the Soul could not have failed to suggest the political tenet that the condition of the commonweal depended absolutely on the will and example of the Prince.

The proliferation of political moralities (especially during the period of religio-political wranglings initiated by Henry VIII's establishing the monarch as head of the church) indicates how readily the analogy was recognized. In these plays, the ground of action becomes more difficult to characterize; it is, roughly, the commonweal, the spirit of the nation, and it is inhabited by personifications of political vices and virtues, as well as by those to which the individual is prey. In *Respublica,* for example, the presence of Insolence and Adulation among the vices points to the shift in focus from health of the soul to health of the nation since they primarily corrupt relationships among men rather than the spiritual state within one man.

The consequences for the body politic of the presence of such vices must, of course, be presented through their interaction with characters representative of the nation as well as with personifications of individual and political virtues. But, although the focus is upon action worked out by characters who, despite their abstract labels, behave like courtiers, prelates, merchants, and farmers, ultimate responsibility for the return to order is always the ruler's. Should he be himself corrupt,

15. For an excellent description of the allegorical logic of the morality plays, see the "Introduction" to Edgar T. Schell and J. D. Shuchter, eds., *English Morality Plays and Moral Interludes.*

even if consequences beyond the "court" are not depicted, the formal given supplies the assumption that the commonweal is consequently in decay. While his individual corruption is deplored, it is deplored primarily because it effects that decay not, as in the pure morality, because of the loss of the individual soul. In understanding the influence of the political moralities on the significant form of later plays, perhaps no assumption of theirs is more important than this: Whether the prince occupies the central role, as in Bale's *King John,* or enters to set things right at the end, as Mary Tudor-Nemesis does in *Respublica,* his presence in the play always formally suggests his affective relationship with the commonweal.

As Wilson's study of Falstaff implies and as E. M. W. Tillyard convincingly demonstrates in *Shakespeare's History Plays,* the assumption of this affective relationship continues to inform the history plays. Although the action in these plays necessarily works itself out through a focus on the central character (or characters), the deeper significance of that action always depends upon the awareness that the fate of a ruler is not a single fate, that his will and action dictate the health of the commonweal.

Certainly, the continuing anxiety and the frenzy of grief expressed by Henry IV in Part 2 (4. 5. 120–38) over Hal's apparent reprobation are not simply those of a father over his son. Sympathetic though that might be, Henry's anguish takes its fearful power from his assumption that because Hal has become riotous, riot will rule at his accession:

> O my poor kingdom, sick with civil blows!
> When that my care could not withhold thy riots,
> What wilt thou do when riot is thy care?
> O, thou wilt be a wilderness again,
> Peopled with wolves, thy old inhabitants![16]

I do not think there can be any question of Shakespeare's perspective on this speech; the resolution of the action clearly ratifies its principles. Hal's conversion is the valid and valued conclusion to the two plays precisely because they are continually informed by the same assumptions as the speech about the

16. *The Complete Plays and Poems of William Shakespeare,* The New Cambridge Edition, eds. William Allan Neilson and Charles Jarvis Hill, 2 *Henry IV,* p. 699. All citations from Shakespeare's plays are from this edition and will henceforth be followed only by act, scene, and line reference.

affective relationship between ruler and ruled.

The degree to which this assumption informs the action of the tragedies of Elizabethan and Jacobean England seems to me definitive of their genres. While a detailed schematization of exclusive categories of tragedy is probably neither possible nor profitable, I think there is some profit in examining the dichotomy in Renaissance tragedy relative to that assumption.

On the one hand, we have tragedies whose primary concern is the individual.[17] The action is circumscribed by, and works itself out in, a sphere defined by the personal, social, or professional relationships of the protagonist. Thus, although Othello is a general and responsible for order in the Venetian army, his generalship is important to the action only to the degree that it helps characterize him, structures his relationship with Iago and Cassio, and lends a certain consequence to the action that it would not, obviously, have if he were a private and his wife a farmer's daughter. I oversimplify, of course, but the point is that Othello's role as general is incidental rather than central to the play. His role as husband is the definitive one. We concern ourselves throughout with the destruction that Iago and he will bring down on his own and Desdemona's heads, with their suffering and his loss, and, in a not simply religious sense, with Othello's individual salvation, not with the consequence of his actions for Venice.

On the other hand, we have plays in which the temperament, attitudes, desires, and, finally, the actions of the protagonist also produce the dramatic conflict which initiates and sustains the action; yet that action is not circumscribed by personal, social, or professional relationships, nor can it be confined to the spheres defined by them. Because the protagonist is either a ruler or at odds with a ruler and because these plays assume the absolute affective relationship between ruler and ruled, the conflict once initiated inevitably spreads outward until it engulfs the commonweal. As in the political moralities, even if these consequences are not presented dramatically, the formal assumption implies them, and, almost invariably, speeches, al-

17. See Henry Hitch Adams, *English Domestic or Homiletic Tragedy*. Adams distinguishes between Domestic and Orthodox tragedy on a basis somewhat similar to mine. Yet, since his emphasis in Domestic tragedy is largely religious, it seems to me that it cannot include a play like *Othello*. As I said, I am not interested in attempting a definitive categorization of Renaissance tragedy, only in defining commonweal tragedy by contrast.

lusions, or references second that implication. Thus, while we are absorbed with Hamlet's personal grief and embattled conscience, Shakespeare reminds us constantly that because of his rank, the prince's actions cannot be regarded as single. Ironically, Shakespeare allows Laertes to admonish Ophelia with what is, despite the speaker, true of Hamlet's predicament:

> For on his choice depends
> The sanity and health of the whole state:
> And therefore must his choice be circumscrib'd
> Unto the voice and yielding of that body—
> Whereof he is the head.

> (1. 3. 20–24)

With deeper irony, he gives to Rosencrantz a speech that condemns the usurper-king it is intended to flatter:

> The cease of majesty
> Dies not alone, but, like a gulf, doth draw
> What's near it, with it. It is a massy wheel,
> Fixed on the summit of the highest mount,
> To whose huge spokes ten thousand lesser things
> Are mortis'd and adjoin'd; which, when it falls
> Each small annexment, petty consequence,
> Attends the boisterous ruin. Never alone
> Did the King sigh, but with a general groan.

> (3. 3. 15–23)

This man who occupies the throne has poisoned Denmark with the dram he poured in the rightful king's ear. When he becomes king, he is at once source and symbol of his country's corruption.[18] Something *is* rotten in the state of Denmark; the time *is* out of joint; and the price of setting it right will be mortal. Yet Hamlet recognizes that he was "born" to that task. He does not bemoan his fate simply as being in the wrong place at the wrong time. It is not the fact of his being born but of the rank into which he was born and, consequently, his relationship to the commonweal that dictate his responsibility.

Significantly, at the end, when he has finally decided that there is a divinity that shapes our ends and that he will, at last, act to avenge his father's death, he does not speak of old Hamlet as his father:

18. In this he is, of course, analogous to Richard III, and from a political standpoint, Hamlet's mandate is as apparent as Monmouth's in *Richard III.*

> He that hath kill'd *my king* and whor'd my mother,
> *Popp'd in between th' election and my hopes,*
> Thrown out his angle for my proper life,
> And with such cozenage—is't not perfect conscience
> To quit him with this arm? And is't not to be damn'd
> To let *this canker of our nature* [my emphases] come
> In further evil?

(5. 2. 64–70)

Of Hamlet's justifications, the larger number are politically normative. Claudius has killed his "king" and kept from the throne one whose claim is not merely lineal but moral. Finally, Hamlet accepts the royal imperative expressed in the royal plural, the prince's responsibility to purge *"our* nature" of this canker. In other words, he will perform the function politically sanctioned and dramatically demanded of him—to restore order, to cleanse the commonweal.

Unfortunately (and for rhetorical and thematic reasons I do not wish to dwell on here), Hamlet may achieve this only with the cease of his own majesty, and his death leaves a dangerous void. If Fortinbras's "election" is to be other than, yet another, usurpation, it must be legitimized by Hamlet's "voice." Yet, all the courtiers had cried "Treason" when Hamlet struck the avenging blow. Shakespeare makes his concern with this political question evident in the care he takes to imply that Horatio's story will not only clear Hamlet's "wounded name" in the world of the play but will prevent further "mischance on plots and errors" from defeating the order so dearly restored by Hamlet's action.

Thus, the play goes beyond Hamlet's fate to concern itself with the fate of the commonweal. Because the broadest emphasis in this genre to which I believe *Hamlet* belongs is characteristically upon the relationship between ruler and ruled, I think *commonweal tragedy* is a convenient term for distinguishing it from the kinds of tragedy whose emphasis is on the individual.

A second generic feature of this category of tragedy, which has its analogues in the morality drama and political doctrine, grows out of the first and, like it, is essential to an understanding of the genre's set on the world. When the will in a morality opts for vice instead of virtue, there is a consequence beyond the obvious one that the ground of the play, the soul, is then in a state of sin: In this perverted state, evil becomes the norm,

and good, as the antithesis of that norm, may, and must logically, be treated as an aberration.

The early sixteenth-century morality *Youth* presents this
neatly in a bit of allegorical action. After Youth has decided to
follow the enticements of Riot instead of the admonitions of
Charity, he tells his Vice of the annoyance he suffered from
Charity's remonstrances and his dread that Charity will return
to chide him again. Riot reassures him:

> Let him come, if he will!
> He were better to bide still.
> And he give thee crooked language,
> I will lay him on the visage;
> And that thou shalt see soon,
> How lightly it shall be done.
> And he will not be ruled with knocks,
> We shall set him in the stocks
> To heal his sore shins.[19]

Later, when Charity does return, Riot and Pride carry out this
threat, and Charity finds himself chained up like a felon.

Ironic it may be to see Charity treated as a criminal, but given
the theology informing this action, it is perfectly reasonable,
and the dramatist takes rhetorical advantage of that irony.
Youth has turned from *caritas* to *cupiditas;* youthful will has
embraced good times rather than Good. Thus, his soul is in a
state of sin; the ground of the play is fallen, ruled by vice
instead of virtue. Obviously, Charity has no recourse, no higher
authority to which he can appeal. In this state controlled by an
obdurately sinful will, right may be wronged. His only hope is
that Youth may undergo a conversion.

The political analogy here is obvious and striking. There is a
convincing circularity in the playwright's choice of this representational feature as metaphor in action. In trying to find an
"analogy of corporeal things"[20] to clothe his abstract argument,
he lights upon the mis-use of this "punitive furniture" of the
judicial system as immediately suggestive. The plight of Charity resembles the plight of many good men who have attempted

19. *The Interlude of Youth,* in Schell and Shuchter, *English Morality Plays and Moral
Interludes,* p. 151, ll. 295–303. All citations from morality dramas contained
herein refer to this edition and will henceforth be referred to by act, scene, and
line numbers.

20. This phrase from an unpublished manuscript of Walter Hilton's is quoted
by A. P. Rossiter in *English Drama from Early Times to the Elizabethans,* p. 79.

to counsel wayward and willful princes. When the prince whose laws and power should guarantee the execution of justice is himself lawless, or has given his power to unjust men, the innocent and virtuous may be victimized by the summary injustice of the powerful.

Taking their cue from just such metaphors as this one in *Youth,* the political dramatists often put the morality form to the purpose of expressing this doctrinal assumption. It was the formal given of the political moralities that if the ruler figure were deceived or indifferent about the nature of evil counsellors, and handed over or allowed them to administer his government, justice could not be found in the nation. *Respublica* provides a clear example of this given. After Avarice, Insolence, Oppression, and Adulation present themselves to Respublica as Policy, Authority, Reformation, and Honesty, respectively, she gives over the governance of the nation to them:

> I like well this trade of Administration!
> Policy for to devise for my commodity,
> No person to be advanced but Honesty,
> Then Reformation good wholesome laws to make
> And Authority see the same effect may take,
> What commonweal shall then be so happy as I?
>
> (2. 2. 521–26)

Of course, the effect of their true nature is as immediately felt by the nation, as it is immediately revealed to the audience through the horseplay and bragging they engage in among themselves. Repeatedly, People comes to Respublica to complain of the Vices' government, and repeatedly, they deceive her into believing that they are devising what they can "for the prosperity / Of this lady, Respublica, and her people" (4. 3. 1039–40). In good faith, she passes along their lying promises and reassurances to People, but he has felt the consequences of their misrule and is not deceived by their projections of a rosy future.

Intimidated by the fear of losing her ministers, Respublica admits to him that "I put trust in other" (4. 3. 1078). Regardless of the evidence of wrongdoing that People brings forth and the justice of his accusations, he has no hope of redress as long as these Vices remain in control. Respublica leaves him in the hands of her ministers for "good counsel," and, from what follows, it is evident that where Vice rules, Virtue is treated as a seditious and rebellious wretch. They accuse him of murmuring against the law, meddling with the high matters that are his betters' affairs, and they warn him:

> INSOLENCE: If thou do so again, it shall with thee be worse.
>   AVARICE: We shall wring and pinch thee both by belly and purse.
> INSOLENCE: I would advise you, friend, to grunt and groan no more.
>   AVARICE: Do the like again and thou shalt rue it full sore.
>
>   (4. 4. 1196–99)

This allegorical action underlines formally how absolutely without recourse People is, but, more importantly, it insists on the total suppression of justice that results from such a situation.

Because this is allegory, when Misericordia appears at the opening of Act 5, we are to understand that through God's mercy the commonweal is to be restored. Yet, even though Truth, Justice, and Peace apprehend, expose, and try the vices for what they are, the action makes clear that justice is only effective through the power of the prince. At the end of Act 5, Scene 9, Justice puts the offenders into People's hands while she, the other Virtues, and Respublica go to fetch Lady Nemesis (who, the Prologue tells us, is Queen Mary) because as Truth had explained:

>   The punishment of this
> Must be referred to the goddess Nemesis.
> She is the most high goddess of correction,
> Clear of conscience and void of affection,
> She hath *power* from above, and is newly sent down
> To redress all outrages in city and town.
> She hath *power* from God all practice to repeal
> Which might bring annoyance to Lady Commonweal.
> *To her office belongeth the proud to overthrow,*
> And such to restore as injury hath brought low.
> 'Tis her *power* [my emphases] to forbid and punish in all estates
> All presumptuous immoderate attemptates.
>
>   (1903–14)

The speech continues, but the important point has been made: Justice must appeal to Lady Nemesis, the ruler of the commonweal, because without the power of the prince, she can effect no change. Justice, in other words, is apparent, despite law and power, but only when backed by law and power is it real.

This assumption is taken over by both the history plays and commonweal tragedy and is often revealed in actions that are formally reminiscent of the moralities. These actions are, of course, representational rather than allegorical in the later plays, but their presence evokes the assumptions informing them and, thus, shapes the rhetorical perspective of the plays. Once again, Henry IV provides a perfect example. The exchange between Falstaff and the Lord Chief Justice (Part 2, Act 1, Scene 2) certainly derives much of its point from its similarity to many such exchanges between vice and virtue in the morality drama. Flippant though he is, Falstaff still has to fear the Lord Chief Justice because Henry IV still reigns, and while he reigns, law and power are fully behind the administration of justice. Yet, the Lord Chief Justice fears that when Hal becomes king, as the chief symbol of Henry's justice, he will have even more to fear from Falstaff because of the latter's influence over the prince.

Once, when arrested for his riotous ways, Hal had struck the Lord Chief Justice who consequently imprisoned him for breaking the king's law. When Henry dies, the Chief Justice dreads that in retribution he will himself be imprisoned. This is an act that he fears more for its political significance than for his own person. His incarceration would be symbolic proof that because its king placed his private desires above the law, England had become a state in which justice is suppressed that lawlessness may rule. Falstaff's response when he learns of Hal's accession bears out the legitimacy of these fears and, again, validates Hal's conversion as the proper conclusion to the two Henry IV plays:

> I am Fortune's steward. . . . Let us take any man's
> horses; the laws of England are at my commandment.
> Blessed are they that have been my friends and woe to my
> Lord Chief Justice.

> (5. 3. 135–45)

The rhetorical effect of this assumption of the ruler's responsibility for ensuring justice in commonweal tragedy is evidenced in King Lear. Lear may excuse himself on the grounds that he is but a foolish, fond old man, more sinned against than sinning, but informed as it is by this assumption, the play puts his responsibility for the action in a somewhat different light.

Cornwall's stocking of Kent (Act 2, Scene 2), given its similarity to Charity's fate in *Youth*, immediately suggests itself in this connection, since Kent is surely a good man and his "crime" is insistence upon the old king's prerogatives. But, unlike Charity, Kent does provoke his punishment by aggressively indecorous action. Nevertheless, his is prefigurative of the fate of virtue and innocence in this kingdom in which power is now in the hands of those who put their wills above justice.

For an audience accustomed to recognizing the assumptions informing the genre, the juxtaposition of the two trial scenes at the end of Act 3 takes on a normative significance that might otherwise be missed. In a hovel adjoining Gloucester's castle, the dispossessed and maddened Lear brings his absent daughters to "trial." His tribunal consists of a bedlam beggar and a fool. He wants Goneril and Regan tried for hardness of heart, and the evident justice of his complaint brings tears to Edgar's eyes. But that is all it can bring about. Once again we see the venerable assumption given dramatic form: In Lear's "court" justice is apparent, but because he has given the power that should enforce that justice to his vicious daughters and their husbands, it is not real.

Immediately following this trial, Regan and Cornwall also set up a tribunal in which they claim to bring Gloucester to justice. His crime is having provided the helpless, mad old king with shelter from a tempest. To Cornwall, this basic act of charity is evidence of conspiracy and treason. He and Regan accuse, judge, and summarily execute sentence upon him. The injustice of this proceeding is patent, and Shakespeare underlines it with a hand that some have seen as heavy. Yet, the sensationalism of Gloucester's blinding is not simply evidence that Shakespeare, too, was inured to the violence that characterized his age or, more cynically, willing to capitalize on it; it has its ethical and rehtorical point. By placing his private desire and his willful choice above his public responsibility and the weal of his kingdom, Lear has created the conditions in which virtue is "vice" and an act of charity a felony. The blinded Gloucester becomes the dramatic symbol of this perversion, a continuing reminder that justice is only a word unless embodied in law and enforced by the power of government.

Shakespeare goes even further to insist on this in the killing of Cornwall's servant. Outraged by the inhumanity of Cornwall's proceedings, the servant attempts to stop the execution and, in so doing, to enact the role of justice. He does manage to wound Cornwall, but, and more to Shakespeare's point, he is immediately run through from behind by Regan, and the execution goes on. In this action, Shakespeare clearly implies that *individual justice* is a contradiction in terms. By giving power to the unjust, Lear has thwarted the operation of justice—except as chance retribution.

How absolutely the play assumes the consequent and virtual reprobation of the kingdom is evidenced in Albany's response to the news of Goneril's and Regan's treatment of their father:

> If that the heavens do not their visible spirits
> Send quickly down to tame these vile offenses,
> It will come
> Humanity must perforce prey on itself
> Like monsters of the deep.

> (4. 3. 46–50)

Ironically, there could be no deeper indictment of Lear because this speech reveals that there is no longer within this kingdom any power for ensuring justice. That power was and should have remained Lear's. His will destroyed the weal of the nation and banished justice along with Cordelia. If the consequences seem inordinately out of proportion to their cause, we are ignoring those generic assumptions concerning his relationship to the commonweal and the inevitability that evil, once loosed through his choice, will transform the nation into a simulacrum of itself.

These two assumptions are that part of Webster's heritage of political dramaturgy that basically informs commonweal tragedy, the genre in which I place *The Duchess of Malfi.* They are definitive of that set upon the world about which, as Colie argued, a great deal need not be said once it has been understood. When the opening of a play established that the central character was a prince whose actions were to be represented seriously and to whose rule there was a threat, either internal or external to himself, these generic assumptions would immediately invoke that set and, thus, impose the values against which those actions were to be judged.

I do not mean to imply by this that all of the plays in this genre are "about" the affective relationship between ruler and ruled, that this is some sort of platonic ideal to which they all aspire. Obviously, each play is about itself, expresses its unique meaning through its dramatic action. This relationship and certain normative attitudes toward it simply provide an orientation that enables us to identify the genre of a play and that creates certain expectations about the direction the play's action will take and about the rhetorical perspective informing that action.

There are certain features which invoked that set more immediately and elliptically than others because they, too, had come forward from the morality drama along with these basic assumptions. For one: In the battle, actual or potential, for the Mankind figure, the vices and virtues both operated on the principle that contiguity with vice automatically corrupts and that constant association with virtue was the only precaution against that corruption. Given the logic of allegory, contiguity with vice necessarily implied temptation, and association with it to the exclusion of virtue represented the fall from grace into sin. How readily this suggested the susceptibility of princes to bad counsellors and favorites and the necessity that the prince provide himself with good counsellors has already been noted in my quotation from Ribner. Thus, for audiences of the histories or commonweal tragedy, to see the prince associated with evil favorites or counsellors was to be immediately attuned to the peril for his own moral and political probity and for that of the nation. As Falstaff says, "Pitch defiles," and an awareness of this convention gives proper weight to the nobility's response to favorites in such plays as *Edward II* and *Richard II*, a response that otherwise often seems to modern students hysterical and picayune.

The rhetorical effect of this feature was reinforced in no small measure by two other conventions impelled out of the theology informing the morality drama and seconded by the lessons of history and political theory. The first was that evil necessarily presented itself as good. No man consciously seeks evil. His error lies in preferring his good to Good. In the moralities, this venerable tenet of Christian theology often took form in the disguises and name changing of the vices, such as I noted in *Respublica.* Obviously, Respublica would not prefer Avarice, but she can be fooled or fool herself out of desperation into accepting Avarice as Policy. In the representational drama of the period, this convention manifests itself *not* in such obvious and mechanical deceptions as Goneril and Regan practice on Lear at the beginning of the play, but in his self-deception about the real nature of his desires and the consequences they will have for the commonweal. Even more darkly, it shows itself in the spectacle of Macbeth consciously weighing all the sanctified reasons against his killing Duncan and still pursuing his own good, his desire to be king.

Man's tendency to believe he is in control of this evil that has become his good is presented in the moralities through a second convention, the metaphor of master and servant. The moralities never tired of dramatizing the truism that we deceive ourselves if we believe we can master our vices; we inevitably end by serving them. Repeatedly, the morality plays demonstrated this by having the Vice offer his services to the Mankind figure or, as in *Respublica,* to the spirit of the nation, only to gain control over the one he pretended to serve. This is presented beautifully in *Mundus et Infans* when Manhood halfheartedly accepts Folly as his servant, placing certain restrictions on him in order that Folly not bring him into shame. Before the end of the play, Folly is helping Manhood "disguise" himself as Shame and leading his "master" to London where he may better teach him to be a fool.

Those who have argued that Hal's "I know you all" speech destroys dramatic tension in *Henry IV* might want to reconsider it in light of this convention. Hal believes he may make his association with vice serve his ultimate purposes; Renaissance audiences accustomed to just this misplaced self-confidence in countless protagonists of the moralities might, as a matter of fact, expect just the reverse. Certainly such audiences could not help but recognize as self-delusion Macbeth's belief that he can make the evil represented by the witches serve him in his conquest of the throne. Once accepted, evil escapes all limits, as Scotland learns to its sorrow, and Scotland is only saved when the evil that Macbeth had hoped would serve him masters him and tricks him into becoming the agent of his own destruction.

There is one last convention of commonweal tragedy that appears extremely mechanical in representational drama, so mechanical that instances of it are often cut in modern productions. Yet, this convention not only implies the broader focus on the commonweal that I see as definitive of the genre, but acts as a kind of rhetorical touchstone in the plays in which it appears. Because the ground of the play in the political moralities was roughly the spirit of the nation, the playwrights adopted certain strategies in order to show the consequences for the commonweal of corruption of that spirit. Obviously, seeing or learning of the consequences of "vicious" choice has more rhetorical weight than simply watching the process by which vice gains control. As my earlier discussion of *Respublica* implied, one convention that grew out of this situation was the introduction of characters who represented the people—the merchants, farmers, and laborers—hardest hit by the corruption of government. The resolution of the action implies how seriously the play intends People's report of the consequences to be taken. As I indicated above, the plight is so dire that it calls down God's mercy, Misericordia, to begin the process of redemption.

These characters might be designated vox populi figures because they represent or speak for the common people concerning the pernicious consequences of bad government. The history plays and commonweal tragedy take them over and use them as such. The father and son of *Henry VI* (Part 3, Act 2, Scene 5); the citizens (Act 2, Scene 3) and the scrivener (Act 3, Scene 6) of *Richard III;* the gardener of *Richard II* (Act 3, Scene 4); Lennox and another lord of *Macbeth* (Act 2, Scene 6); the servants of *King Lear* (Act 3, Scene 7); and, as we shall see, the pilgrims (Act 3, Scene 4) and the officers (Act 2, Scene 2) of *The Duchess of Malfi* all provide examples. Obviously, playwrights in the representational mode have other means available to them for showing consequences: For example, we see the murder of Lady Macduff and her children, the swaggering of Oswald, the fate of Hastings, all the result of evil rule. Such possibilities make the continuing use of these vox populi figures provocative —unless we are to dismiss them as merely vestigial, conventional throwbacks to the earlier drama. To me, they represent at least three factors: a traditional urge toward conceptualization in the drama, an economical means of insisting on the degree to which the sins of the great are apparent to and consequential for all members of the commonweal, and a generic signpost. When these characters appeared, the audience of commonweal tragedy could expect their report to represent the play's evaluative perspective on princely actions. We ignore them at our critical peril.

These, then, are some of the assumptions and conventions that are part of Webster's heritage of political dramaturgy out of which commonweal tragedy is formed. The values, concerns, and sense of purpose of the plays in this genre express the political idealism of Renaissance England. Their characteristic conflict is the tension between private, individual desire in a prince, or those who endanger him, and the weal of the nation. Their characteristic fear is of the chaos that results when such desire takes precedence over the prince's responsibility to ensure that weal through action and example.

As I said earlier, the plays themselves reveal the didactic purpose Sidney claimed for tragedy, to teach kings the necessity for ruling well, but they reveal a wider intention: They are also aimed at the ruled. They never allow the audience to lose sight of the individual's capacity for bringing the world down around everyone's ears. Their presentation of full and compelling individuals is a generic concomitant of the rhetorical thrust that ultimately affirms the values of community, order, degree, and justice in the face of the radical individualism that threatens those values. By presenting protagonists and, very often, villains sympathetically, the playwrights sharpened their rhetorical effects. The sympathy we feel for such characters, the responsive chord they strike in us, indicates to each of us that we contain, at least, the potential for disorder that could, if loosed, destroy the common weal.

In his excellent study of *Macbeth*, Paul Jorgensen describes this as the effect of "sensational art," an art characteristic of Jacobean tragedy. In pointing to "the sublunary, the human" source of the sensational, he speaks of "that part of ourselves which is designed to make us tremble in recognition, through great art, at something disturbingly strange and potentially dangerous within ourselves."[21] This recognition suggests to us that nothing must be done to undermine the institutions that man has erected against his own potential for evil because evil, once unleashed, consumes the guilty and the innocent alike. It cannot be checked until, having consumed everything in its path, it turns upon and consumes itself.

For commonweal tragedy, the primary bulwark against that force is the monarchy. Because of the affective relationship between the prince's will and the weal of the nation, these plays insist repeatedly that he place that weal above his individual will, that he subordinate his personal desires to his public responsibility. He may not be swayed from this duty by those desires and emotions that the rhetoric of the plays has made us

21. Paul Jorgensen, *Our Naked Frailties,* p. 11.

aware of in ourselves. These dicta receive perhaps their most explicit treatment in all of commonweal tragedy in Act 4, Scene 3, of *Macbeth*. In order to test Macduff's integrity, Malcolm paints himself as a compendium of vices. Macduff delivers the normative response when he then withdraws his support of Malcolm's claim to the throne and cries out to his country: "O nation miserable. . . . When shalt thou see thy wholesome days again?"

2. The Immediate Context

Webster or any of his contemporaries living close to the court of King James I might well have asked that same question. The reality of his rule departed so radically from the political ideals informing commonweal tragedy that the genre must have seemed "distinctly old-fashioned" nine years after James's accession, when Webster was writing *The Duchess of Malfi*. James himself in his *Basilikon Doron*, written for the education of his son Prince Henry, duly reiterated all the ideals of princely behavior that are assumed by the genre. Not least among these was the necessity for extraordinary moral probity in a ruler whose every action would be an example for the ruled:

> A moate in another's eye, is a beame into yours: a blemishe in another, is a leprouse byle into you: and a venial sinne . . . in another is a greate crime into you. Thinke not therefore, that the highnes of your dignity diminsheth your faults (much les giueth you a license to sin) but by the contrarie, your fault shalbe aggrauated according to the highte of your dignite, any sin that ye commit not being a single sinne procuring but the fal of one; but being an exemplare sinne, and therefore draweth with it the whole multitude to be guyltie of the same.[22]

Obviously, James understood the ideal. Perhaps, inflated as he was by the rhetoric of address to a divinely sanctioned, absolute monarch, he may have believed he realized that ideal. But history indicates that he more often provided his subjects with evidence that the same passions swayed him as swayed the least of them and that his faults were indeed aggravated according to the height of his "dignity."

King James could counsel his heir to make his "court and companie to bee a pasture of godlenesse and all honeste vertues

22. James I, *Basilikon Doron*, pp. 4–5.

to all the rest of the people,"[23] but contemporary reports imply that James's own court could much more truly be described as Ferdinand describes the Duchess's court—as a "rank pasture." In his study of the *Jacobean Pageant,* G. P. V. Akrigg devotes an informative and illuminating chapter to the "painful discrepancy between theory and practice which King James' subjects could not but observe in looking at their sovereign and his court." He notes that in the opening lines of *The Duchess of Malfi,* Webster supplies "a most eloquent description of the ideal court" but that "indicative of Webster's view of the realities of court life is the fact that in the rest of his play he uses 'court', like many another Englishman, as a term of angry opprobrium."[24] Akrigg describes James's court as characterized by "its extravagant luxury, its unruliness, its sycophancy, and its all-pervasive graft and corruption."[25] Far from providing the corrective ideal exalted by Antonio's speech, political theory, and commonweal tragedy, James's personal and administrative actions provided the example of one who "drank too much, neglected his duties for his pleasures, and exchanged filthy jests with debauched favorites."[26]

On this matter of favorites, James had, once again, provided his son with orthodox advice: "Employe euerie man as ye think him qualified, but use not one in al things, least he waxe proude and be enuyed by his marrowes."[27] But, again, he proved himself unable to practice his orthodox preaching. According to M. M. Reese, the effect of his absolute reliance on favorites was disastrous to the morale and the morality of his administrators:

> Men who had known Leicester and Essex were well enough accustomed to court favorites, but Elizabeth had seldom allowed her private affections to direct public policy. James made no such distinctions, the favorite's whim was his master's law. Experienced statesmen took their orders from Somerset and Buckingham, and did them homage for favours expected and received.[28]

23. Ibid., p. 83.
24. G. P. V. Akrigg, *Jacobean Pageant or The Court of King James I,* p. 227, and see pp. 245–47 for a discussion of flattery as a "courtly" form in James's reign.
25. Ibid., p. 228.
26. Ibid., p. 246.
27. James I, *Basilikon Doron,* p. 85.
28. Reese, *The Tudors and Stuarts,* p. 161.

What underscored James's weakness and irresponsibility in failing to provide standards and maintain discipline was a tactless and unrelenting insistence on his divine right to rule and on his supreme authority over all men. This insistence could hardly have failed to exacerbate his subjects' painful awareness of how far from ideal was this man whose will determined the weal of the nation, especially since James was quite capable of acting the part that he himself described as tyrannical in this contrast between the tyrant and a lawful good king:

> The one acknowlegeth himself ordeined for his people, hauing receiued from God a burthen of gouerment whereof he must be countable; The other thinketh his people ordeyned for him, a praye to his appetites. . . . A good King (thinking his highest honor to consist in the due discharge of his calling) employeth all his studie and pains to procure and maintaine (by making and execution of good lawes) the well-fare and peace of his people, and . . . thinketh his greatest contentment standeth in their prosperitie, and his greatest suretie in hauing their hearts, subjecting his owne priuate affections and appetites to the weill and standing of his subjects, euer thinking the common interesse his cheirest particular. . . . Whereby the contrary, an usurping Tyrante . . . counterfaiting the Sainte while he once creepe in credit, will then (by inuerting all good lawes to serue only his unrulie priuate affections) forme the common-weale euer to advance his particular.[29]

From the number of incidents in which James acted the tyrant rather than the good king, his subjects might well have begun to wonder if it were possible for him—or any king—to place the "common-weale" above his private affections and appetites. For a brief period, they apparently looked forward with hope to the day when Prince Henry might lead the country to health and greatness again. Ironically, James's son seems to have taken every word of *Basilikon Doron* to heart and improved upon it. Opinion held, and still holds, that he was everything a king should be and, thus, everything that his father was not. Looking at his virtues and his abilities, the people of England could again believe in the possibility that from a prince's court might flow "pure silver drops" of good example and good governance.

Unfortunately, Henry died. Akrigg describes the reaction:

29. James I, *Basilikon Doron*, pp. 28–30.

The shock of Henry's death brought home to the English how much they had built their expectations upon him. . . . As the court of his father became more and more recognized for the lax, spendthrift ill-disciplined thing it was, the English had increasingly either looked back nostalgically to the great days under Elizabeth or had promised themselves future greatness under King Henry. In the high idealism of the young prince had been something that appealed to all that was good in his age. When he died the grief of the nation was commensurate with its sense of loss.[30]

That grief and sense of loss must have been terribly aggravated by the grim awareness that there was no likelihood that James and his court would ever be other than they were and that the nation was stuck with them. The death of hope would add significantly to the anguish of the upright and the cynicism of the corrupt.

All in all, the ideals of political theory and commonweal tragedy seemed to be given the lie by the reality of King James's monarchy. The affective relationship between ruler and ruled that should guarantee the common weal became instead, in the eyes of many, a patent threat to it. It seems to me that *Hamlet, Lear,* and *Macbeth* imply a kind of fear that this might be true, but by the time of Henry's death, plays such as *Coriolanus, Troilus and Cressida, The White Devil,* and *The Revenger's Tragedy* simply assume that it is true.

How then, and why, would Webster return to a genre informed by ideals so spectacularly ignored in the context in which he was writing? All around him, he could certainly see negative illustrations of the political doctrine and the rhetorical perspective informing the earlier drama. Repeatedly, the culpable actions of James and his court had the sorts of consequences for the commonweal that these traditions had insisted that such actions would have. The answer seems to be that, as I said earlier, in such a context, this genre obviously took on considerable ironic significance.

At this late date in the genre's history and in a political context such as Antonio's opening speech describes, or that the court of King Henry might have provided, Webster might well have had to parody the conventions in order to appear other than hopelessly imitative and unoriginal. He would have been in a position analogous to that of the Petrarchan sonneteer at the end of the sixteenth century. As Sidney, for example, was aware, if a gentleman wished to praise his lady with a sonnet, his sincerity would be highly questionable should he reveal all the conventional assumptions, use all the conventional images, and strike all the conventional poses. Only by parodying the conventions, seriously or comedically, could he make them a significant means of individual expression, and avoid satirizing himself as lover and as poet.[31]

On the other hand, say that the sonneteer's intention were satiric, that he wished to point up the ironic nature of his flattery or the unworthiness of its object, then, the straightest, most single-mindedly conventional use of the form would accomplish his purpose economically. Webster's situation is more nearly analogous to this. No variation, no inversion, was needed to give the genre experiential significance. He could use the conventions of commonweal tragedy without parody because its every convention and assumption stood as a grim indictment of the world mirrored by the world of the play.[32]

Berry contends that in *The Duchess of Malfi*, "the positive values are human, not religious. No extra-subjective reality is seriously advanced."[33] If among human values he includes political values, I would agree with the first statement, but not with the second. Because of the ideals informing it and the generic expectations it raises, the genre itself advances that extra-subjective reality. It implies the values of political order: The responsibility of rulers for the common weal and the necessity for law to embody, and power to enforce, justice—if justice is to be more than an abstraction.

Because Webster made his protagonist a woman, it might be argued that he was violating the audience's generic expectation that the prince would be a man and that he was thereby expressing his sense that the ideal relationship between ruler and ruled could not be realized. As Lagarde says in his marvelously comprehensive study of Webster, "for an Elizabethan or a Jacobean a woman or a child is admirable only to the degree that

31. For a discussion of this aspect of the sonneteer's dilemma and the critical question of parody as serious comment on form see Murray Krieger, *A Window to Criticism*. See also, Wayne Booth, *A Rhetoric of Irony*, pp. 123–34.

32. Satire is not my primary concern in this study, nor, I think, was it Webster's. The satiric aspect of the play simply provides yet another ironic turn to its rhetorical perspective. Unlike many of his critics Webster does not assume that because the object of his satire violated political ideals, the ideals are invalidated.

33. Berry, *The Art of John Webster*, p. 128.

the woman or the child recalls the man."[34] Webster's Duchess rarely recalls the man. She is very much a woman, and according to medieval and Renaissance tradition, a woman was made to be ruled, not to rule. Thus, in making his ruler a woman, Webster would seem to be loading the dice. Indeed, some might argue that, since there is speculation that Webster was a Puritan, following his spiritual leader John Knox, he might believe that it is "more than monstrous to have a woman reign over men."[35] If Webster held these views, the Duchess's downfall would be a given.

It is, finally, not to my purpose to argue whether or not Webster believed that the ideal of government could any longer be realized or whether or not he was a Puritan. Regardless of where he stood on these matters, I do not think that in Webster's eyes, the Duchess's sex would automatically have disallowed her from realizing that ideal. The men of Webster's era were, after all, quite accustomed to the reign of women. Elizabeth had demonstrated beyond a doubt that a woman could rule at least as well as any man. She had repeatedly managed to subordinate her personal desires to her public responsibility, and, as Akrigg's remarks on the response to Henry's death indicated, by the time Webster was writing *The Duchess of Malfi*, a great many Englishmen were looking back nostalgically to her reign as a golden age. At this point they had the son of Mary Queen of Scots on the throne, and while Mary's career might seem to attest to the inability of women to rule, it was not because of her sex that the Scots forced her to abdicate nor that Englishmen feared her claim to the English crown.

As I said earlier, Mary's downfall must have looked to both friends and foes like a precise charting of the consequences for ruler and ruled when a prince places his will above the weal of his nation. Lagarde, among others, has noted that the Duchess's story could not but recall Mary's problems to the minds of Webster's contemporaries, and this memory might well have been refreshed by the notorious matter of Lady Arabella Stuart. Since 1610, King James had kept this cousin of his imprisoned in the Tower for secretly marrying—without his consent and in defiance of his wishes—a man who was beneath her in rank.

34. Fernand Lagarde, *John Webster*, p. 838, my translation (with due apologies to Professor Lagarde).

35. John Knox, quoted in Camden, *The Elizabethan Woman*, p. 252, and Einstein, *Tudor Ideals*, p. 90.

Lady Arabella apparently shared the Stuart "luck," and since the cause of her downfall was an unwise marriage, her predicament surely recalled Mary's spectacular unwisdom in marriage.[36]

The similarities between Mary and the Duchess are striking to the point that it would seem unrealistic to dismiss them as wholly coincidental. Mary was beautiful, charming, witty, imprudent, passionate, and willful, and so is the Duchess. Both of them married in defiance of political realities and reputation. Because of her subsequent loss of reputation, the Pope seizes the dukedom that the Duchess held as dowager and abandons her to the custody of her brother. Because of the scandalous nature of Mary's marriage to Bothwell, Pius V refused to have any further communication with her unless he should see "some better sign of her life and religion than he has witnessed in the past."[37] As a further result of her questionable repute, the Catholic powers of Europe hesitated to attempt rescuing her from Elizabeth's "custody." Besides being imprisoned by their kinsmen, both Mary and the Duchess suffer considerable mental and physical anguish and are at length "executed" with their eyes firmly on heaven. Indeed, the Duchess's final attitude and words are not unlike those of Mary on the scaffold at Fotheringay.

I do not stress these similarities because I want to argue that Webster consciously thought of Mary as an analogue of the Duchess—although I think a convincing case could be made. The similarities are finally more important for another reason: Critics have consistently looked at the Duchess only as a woman and, with incredibly few exceptions, have ignored her political role as completely as though her title and that of the play were not *Duchess* of Malfi, whereas the similarities between her story and Mary's and the generic expectations aroused by

36. See Akrigg, Chapter 11, "The Languishing Lady," pp. 113–24, for the complete account of Lady Arabella's troubles. For further corroboration of her topical interest see G. B. Harrison, *A Second Jacobean Journal: Being a Record of Those Things Most Talked of during the Years 1607 to 1610,* particularly pp. 212–13. William Seymour's birth was the major problem for the lovers but not because of its baseness, rather, because as descendants of royal lines, their marriage would constitute a political union and threat to James. A number of critics, for example Lagarde, *John Webster,* 1:442, have mentioned Lady Arabella's relevance to *The Duchess of Malfi.*

37. Frank Arthur Mumby, *The Fall of Mary Stuart: A Narrative in Contemporary Letters,* p. 250.

commonweal tragedy would have disposed Webster's audience to see her *primarily* as Duchess.

Nine years beyond Elizabeth's reign, with Mary's son as king, Jacobeans could hardly have assumed that her sex should indicate that the Duchess was not to be seen as ruler nor that she need not subordinate her personal desires to her public responsibility. In this, the context of the play, the generic expectations it raises, and the rhetoric informing its structure are mutually reinforcing. In looking at the play, we must judge the Duchess according to her own claim: "For know, whether I am doom'd to live or die, I can do both like a prince."[38]

38. John Webster, *The Duchess of Malfi,* ed. John Russell Brown, p. 78, Act 3, Sc. 2, ll. 70–71. All citations are from this edition and will henceforth be followed by act, scene, and line reference.

3

Into a Wilderness

In the opening of *The Duchess of Malfi*, Webster wastes no time in establishing a standard against which the Duchess's claim may be measured. Responding to Delio's question about the French court, Antonio replies:

> I admire it—
> In seeking to reduce both state and people
> To a fix'd order, their judicious king
> Begins at home: quits first his royal palace
> Of flatt'ring sycophants, of dissolute,
> And infamous persons—which he sweetly terms
> His Master's master-piece, the work of Heaven.
>
> (1. 1. 4–10)

Any number of critics have noted the political orthodoxy of this speech. They accept it as a conventional expression of the Renaissance ideal of government—if not the superlative one that Akrigg deems it. This acceptance, however, rarely amounts to more than dismissal. Rather than seeing it as the establishment of Webster's perspective or set on the action of the play, most critics dutifully discuss its typicality and never refer to it again. Indeed, its relevance to the action is so little recognized that the recent BBC production I spoke of in Chapter 1, simply cut it, and the play opened on Antonio's characters of the Aragonian brothers.[1]

1. See Ian Jack, "The Case of John Webster," p. 42. Jack quotes the second, third, and fourth lines of Antonio's speech, then goes on: "To point the contrast Bosola—who is one of the 'dissolute, and infamous persons' who are banished from any healthy court—enters just as this speech is finished. If Webster were an orthodox Elizabethan, *the rest of the play would be an illustration of what happens in a state of which the Prince himself is evil:* Death and diseases through the whole land spread." Jack's "inattention" is instructive. He sees the orthodoxy of the speech but fails to see how it does provide an illustration *not* of what happens when "the Prince himself is evil" (Antonio's speech says nothing about any inherent evil in the prince), but of what happens when "curs'd example" poisons the common fountain of government near the head. Webster's orthodoxy was apparently too consistent and too Jacobean for Jack to catch. His article is, of course, an extreme example of attacks on the play's structural coherence and rhetorical perspective.

·Yet, given the heritage of political dramaturgy Webster shared with his audience, this opening speech and the ideals it assumes could not have failed to establish Webster's genre and, thus, arouse certain generic expectations. The play opens in a particular court with the description of an ideal court. For Webster's audience the implications, the expectations, and the questions would be obvious: How will the ruler and the court depicted in the action to come measure up to the standard established? Is the prince going to subordinate his will to the weal of his subjects? In this instance, of course, it is *her* will and *her* subjects. After all, this is the court of the dowager Duchess of Malfi, who is responsible for the judicious administration of affairs of this state she is ruling for her son in his minority. What shape will the conflict between ideals of order and individual will assume in this case?

In the lines that follow, Webster not only permits Antonio to continue in his role as spokesman for the ideal but also provides a hint in answer to that last question:

> A prince's court
> Is like a common fountain, whence should flow
> Pure silver drops in general: but if't chance
> Some curs'd example poison't near the head,
> *Death, and diseases through the whole land spread.*

(1. 1. 11–15)

A Renaissance audience would instantly understand the significance of Antonio's analogy of the prince's court as a fountain. It might recall to them Sir Thomas More's trope in *Utopia:* "For the springs of both good and evil flow from the prince, over a whole nation, as from a lasting fountain."[2] But its lineage was venerable, and it had been used to illuminate the ruler-ruled relationship long before its appropriation by medieval political theologians. In Antonio's speech, the focus narrows to the exemplary role of the prince, to the poisonous effect his "exemplare sinne" will have upon the moral and political health of the nation. Webster's audience, who, some have claimed, were better listeners than we, might well have been alerted that in this play the threat to the common weal lay in that direction.

In choosing this venerable trope, Webster certainly places *The*

2. Ligeia Gallagher, ed., *More's UTOPIA and its Critics,* p. 5.

Duchess of Malfi thematically, doctrinally, and conventionally as commonweal tragedy. But his use of it goes beyond the merely conventional: With it he sets up a metaphor of the action to follow, provides a standard against which that action can be charted, and furnishes us with an imagistic Ariadne's thread. By immediately establishing the image of a spreading poison of "death and disease" caused by "curs'd example" and the political significance of that image, he is able to use it as a kind of rhetorical metonomy throughout the play. At crucial points he can evoke the whole framework of political, ethical values and assumptions and invite the audience to bring it to bear upon actions, ideas, or characters simply by using the image he has set up as its counterpart.[3]

At the same time that Webster so economically establishes his set on the action and hints at the source of conflict, he also allows the nature of the speech to give the speaker a certain ethical authority in the audience's eyes. Antonio has an immediate sympathetic edge over the other characters because of the values he holds and the judgments he makes on the basis of them. Webster begins validating Antonio's judgment immediately, for the words concerning the poisonous effect of corruption in princes are scarcely out of his mouth when Bosola enters. Bosola is a living example of that effect. He has been suborned and then deserted by the Cardinal, and as Antonio says, " 'Tis great pity / He should be thus neglected—I have heard / He's very valiant: this foul melancholy / Will *poison* [my emphasis] all his goodness . . ." (1. 1. 74–77).

Through his connection with Bosola, the suggestion is made that the Cardinal is a corrupt and corrupting prince. But in drama, the past is hearsay, and we are concerned with present action. Antonio has made a prediction; and by means of that imagistic echo of poison, the relationship between the quality of rulers and the health of the ruled is kept in mind. The question is: Will the dramatic future second Antonio's judgment about that relationship, and, if so, how?

As Robert Ornstein has pointed out, Bosola is a sort of inverse analogue of Antonio in many ways, and it is interesting

3. See Hereward T. Price, "The Function of Imagery in Webster"; Price explicates the imagery of poison carefully in his article, touching on a number of the same points as I, but his concern is with the imagery as it provides unity in the play, whereas I see the imagistic unity as a manifestation of structural coherence and rhetorical consistency.

to note how often in Act 1 they counterpoint each other in judgment and corroboration.[4] Through Bosola, we will be presented with vivid evidence of the truth of Antonio's claim, and so it is fitting that Bosola should introduce, in a variation on Antonio's imagistic theme, Ferdinand's and the Cardinal's perversion of the normative political relationship:

> He, and his brother, are like plum-trees, that grow crooked over standing pools; they are rich, and o'erladen with fruit, but none but crows, pies, and caterpillars feed on them: could I be one of their flattering panders, I would hang on their ears like a horse-leech till I were full, and then drop off.
>
> (1. 1. 49–54)

Instead of recipients of water flowing from a pure fount of government, those most immediately subject to their rule, their courtiers, are seen here as parasites, living off and sated by "nourishment" suggestive of poisonous superfluity. For Webster's audience, these lines would have an extra-dramatic edge as well. The similarity between these people and the hangers-on of James's court are obvious, and the image is doubly damning in that it is an inversion of lines Webster penned at virtually the same time. In his elegy for Prince Henry, "A Monumental Column," he vaunts Henry's scrupulous moderation and impartiality in images of which Bosola's might be a parody:

> He spread his bounty with a provident hand;
> And not like those that sow th' ingratefull sand.
> His rewards followed reason, nere were plac't
> For ostentation; and to make them last,
> He was not like the mad and thriftlesse Vine,
> That spendeth all her blushes at one time:
> But, like the *Orange* tree, his fruits he bore;
> Some gather'd, he had greene, and blossomes store.[5]

As extensions of Antonio's earlier trope, Bosola's images and metaphors also point to Ferdinand's and the Cardinal's misrule

4. Robert Ornstein, *The Moral Vision of Jacobean Tragedy*, p. 142. More recently, this has been noted by Lois Potter, "Realism Versus Nightmare: Problems of Staging *The Duchess of Malfi*."

5. John Webster, "A Monumental Column," in *The Complete Works of John Webster*, ed. F. L. Lucas, 3:276, ll. 43–46. This poem has been generally mentioned for its interest in connection with *The Duchess* because Webster apparently broke off composing the play in order to write it, and it contains a number of echoes (or prefigurations) of lines in the play which provide some insight into Webster's meanings.

on a number of levels. First of all, the fountain of Antonio's speech flows, is vital, and figuratively makes the benefits of good rule available to all. The "standing pools" of Bosola's speech suggest not only a poisonous stagnation, but a barrier placed between ruler and ruled. The major thrust of Bosola's figure is that Ferdinand's and the Cardinal's "government" hoards up benefits owed to all for the ruler himself and those few whose temperamental and ethical distortions enable them to thrive in such a stagnant environment. Despite Bosola's self-interest, the speech implies that the essence of the brothers' perversion is that they place private indulgence above public weal.

One of the ways in which their radical self-indulgence shows is in their being surrounded by "flattering panders" (recalling the earlier "flatt'ring sycophants") rather than the "provident Council" established as ideal in the last lines of Antonio's opening speech:

> And what is't makes this blessed government,
> But a most provident Council, who dare freely
> Inform him the corruption of the times?
> Though some o'th' court hold it presumption
> To instruct princes what they ought to do,
> It is a noble duty to inform them
> What they ought to foresee.
>
>   (1. 1. 16–22)

Between Antonio's measured and graceful presentation of the ideal and Bosola's carping and satiric portrait of the actuality of the Aragonian brothers' retinue, I cannot help wonder if Webster might have intended, as Hamlet did, to catch the conscience of the king, to mirror the corruption of the times, and to warn him of what he ought to foresee. Be that as it may, Webster hastens to corroborate Bosola's judgment of Ferdinand. In the next scene, a bored Ferdinand is presented in company with Castruchio, Silvio, Roderigo, and Grisolan. He is discussing the tilt, longing after real action, and questioning Castruchio about his wife. The atmosphere and the jokes are decidedly stagnant, but when Silvio makes a joke at Castruchio's expense, and two of the courtiers laugh, Ferdinand reproves them in a manner that clearly bears out the truth of Bosola's perceptions:

> Why do you laugh? Methinks you that are
> courtiers should be my touch-wood, take fire,

when I give fire; that is, laugh when I laugh,
were the subject never so witty.

(1. 1. 122–25)

Apparently, the ruler-ruled relationship assumed by Ferdinand
would make of his subjects no more than automata whose
motive force must be his will. His demonstration not only validates Bosola's indictment but makes the character that Antonio
will paint of the Duke and Cardinal at Delio's request doubly
ominous.

At the heart of Antonio's assessment of both of them is an
accusation that, besides putting their private desires above the
common weal, they use the very institutions that should guarantee that weal to undermine it. Antonio describes the Cardinal
thus:

> He is a melancholy churchman; the spring in his face is nothing
> but the engendering of toads; where he is jealous of any man, he
> lays worse plots for them than ever was imposed on Hercules, for
> he strews in his way flatterers, panders, intelligencers, atheists,
> and a thousand such political monsters. He should have been
> Pope; but instead of coming to it by the primitive decency of the
> church, he did bestow bribes so largely, and so impudently, as if
> he would have carried it away without heaven's knowledge.

(1. 1. 157–66)

In short, he is a prince of the Church who seeks to destroy souls
rather than save them and who would subvert that very Church
in order to become, and by becoming, its head. His private
desire for power so takes precedence over the common weal
that he would corrupt the institutions whose spiritual guidance
should lead men to sanctity, individually and communally.
What makes this doubly sinister is that the Church is a State
that subsumes other states, spiritually; thus, as prince of the
Church, he is a threat to many commonweals.

As the Cardinal misuses his spiritual authority, the Duke
misuses his legal authority, according to the exchange between
Antonio and Delio:

> *Ant.* The duke there? a most perverse, and turbulent nature:
>   What appears in him mirth, is merely outside;
>   If he laugh heartily, it is to laugh
>   All honesty out of fashion. . . .
>   He speaks with others' tongues, and hears men's suits
>   With others' ears; will seem to sleep o'th' bench

> Only to entrap offenders in their answers;
> Dooms men to death by information,
> Rewards by hearsay.

Delio.   Then the law to him
> Is like a foul black cobweb to a spider—
> He makes it his dwelling, and a prison
> To entangle those shall feed him.

Ant.   Most true:
> He ne'er pays debts, unless they be shrewd turns,
> And those he will confess that he doth owe.

(1. 1. 169–82)

By focusing on the Cardinal's perversion of religion and Ferdinand's corruption of the law, Webster very elliptically, in contemporary terms, implies the broader and more serious effect of their rule. From the standpoint of Renaissance political theory, they strike at the bases of government:

> Religion can not be entertained, if it be not backt with ciuill Iustice, which reciprocallie hath need of deuout pietie: for the Religio is iust, and iustice of it self, is holy and religious: so thei are the two estates which the Scripture names the tru foundacions and pillors of comon weales.[6]

Thus, between them these twins "in quality" would subvert religion and justice, the true foundations of commonweals. Obviously, this is worse than "curs'd example" that poisons the common fountain. These princes are virtual sources of corruption, and, almost immediately, we see the poisonous effect they have on those subject to their influence. Ferdinand corrupts Bosola, persuades him to employment that Bosola himself describes in terms of filth, corruption, and damnation. In return for Ferdinand's procuring the "provisorship o' the horse" in the Duchess's household for him, Bosola will spy on the Duchess for her brother.[7] The arrangement validates both Antonio's

6. Geoffrey Fenton, *A Form of Christian Pollicie, 1574,* p. ii. I modernize the typography somewhat.

7. See James I, *Basilikon Doron,* pp. 80–81: "Let my example then teach you to follow the rules here set down, choosing your servants for your owne use, and not for the use of others . . . so choose you servants indifferently out of all quarters, not respecting other men's appetites, but their owne qualities." In light of this, the ease with which the Duchess accepts Bosola at Ferdinand's request, when she knows Ferdinand is to be feared, would underline her superficiality as ruler. Her attention is not on the realities of rule but—as we learn—on her private desires, so she placates Ferdinand with a sort of reparation in advance. Fernand Lagarde, in *John Webster,* 2:848, comes down on her very hard for this as evidence of her unfitness to rule.

political theory and his assessment of Ferdinand.

It is interesting to pause and look at the play's perspective on Antonio at this point. His perceptions of character have been corroborated, his ethical and political values presented as normative, and his moral probity attested to almost by the devil himself. Antonio had said of the Cardinal, "They that do flatter him most say oracles / Hang at his lips: and verily I believe them; / For the devil speaks in them" (1. 1. 184–86). Later, when Ferdinand remarks that "Antonio . . . had been far fitter" for the job than Bosola, the Cardinal disagrees: "You are deceiv'd in him / His nature is too honest for such business" (1. 1. 229–30). Obviously, the Cardinal has more insight into human nature than his brother—or has he? Antonio appears to him as he has been made to appear to us, as everything that Bosola (or the Cardinal and Ferdinand) is not. He seems to be the honest steward, the sort of provident counsellor he mentions in his opening speech, a subject whose loyalty is above all ambition or greed. From the standpoint of generic expectations, Antonio would be seen as the perfect servant and perfect counsellor for the Duchess. Herein lies one of Webster's more dramatic ironies and, I think, one of the cruxes of misinterpretation of the values of the play.

It is the very clarity with which Antonio sees the quality of the Duchess's brothers, the very orthodoxy of his political doctrine, and the very loyalty he feels for the Duchess as "great-master of her household" and her counsellor that render him culpable when he capitulates to her wooing and agrees to the secret marriage. He has presented the normative concept of his role, and he himself violates it. He makes only one weak attempt at the noble duty of informing the Duchess of "What [she] ought to foresee." But because she has offered him her "all," her "excellent self," he allows her to put aside his concern about her brothers' reactions with an imperious but naive fiat:

> Do not think of them—
> All discord, without this circumference,
> Is only to be pitied, and not fear'd:
> Yet, should they know it, time will easily
> Scatter the tempest.

$$(1. 1. 468–72)$$

The willful, wishful, imprudence of this would hardly have been lost on Jacobeans. These lines echo only too clearly Mary Stuart's mistaken belief that she could sweep away all dissen-

sion of her lords—especially of her unsympathetic and powerful half-brother, the Earl of Moray—at her marriage to Bothwell. Lady Arabella Stuart's similar belief that once she was
married to William Seymour, her cousin King James would
have to accept it offered too recent an example of wishful
thinking to Webster's audience for these lines to be other than
prophetically foreboding. Aside from such topical considera-
tions, Antonio has described and we have seen enacted the evil
quality and the unscrupulous power of the Duchess's brothers.
Antonio, because he is of lower rank, has no more power than
the Duchess can bestow on him with which to counter the
tempest that her action looses. Thus, his acceptance of her offer
in the face of his own perceptions and pronounced values is not
unlike Bosola's acceptance of a role that he himself describes as
corrupt and corrupting. Generically speaking, the actions of
both are recognizable as manifestations of the truism that man
never seeks evil, but that in preferring his "good" to Good he
falls into sin—in this case, political sin.

Bosola is, understandably, less self-deceived than Antonio,
thus more culpable, and, certainly, Antonio's passion for the
Duchess is a more agreeable "fault" than Bosola's passion for
preferment, but that is beside Webster's point. Both of them
believe that they can make deception serve ultimate ends, and,
in this, they manifest that other generic truism that we deceive
ourselves when we think we can control the vices we employ
to serve us. The structure of the play at this point clearly suggests a similarity of kind, if not degree, in their situations.

If drama is, indeed, the art of significant juxtaposition,[8] I do
not think the effect of juxtaposing the scene of Ferdinand's
"wooing" of Bosola with that of the Duchess's wooing of Antonio can be denied.[9] Only one incident intervenes between the
scene in which Bosola is bought to perform actions that he
characterizes as "all the ill man can invent" and the scene in
which Antonio is "bought" to accept a role that (in the light of
all he has said and we have seen substantiated) convicts him of
being, at the least, an unfit counsellor. The similarity of action
in the two encounters underlines the similarity in quality.

8. H. D. F. Kitto, *Form and Meaning in Drama*, p. 270.

9. See François André Camoin, *The Revenge* [*sic*] *Convention in Tourneur, Webster
and Middleton*, ed. James Hogg, p. 84. Camoin speaks of it as ". . . the seduction
scene (no other word fits it so well) in which he first refuses Ferdinand's money,
then accepts it with full knowledge of what he will have to do to earn it."

In both cases, the ruler sets out to bind the subject in a secret relationship. Both the duke and Duchess move cautiously to sound the subject's receptivity because a too hasty revelation of true intent might expose them to varying degrees of embarrassment or danger. Both subjects demur only to have their reluctance soothed away by a greater insight into the reward offered. Finally, the outcome of both encounters is that the rulers have "purchased" instruments for satisfying private desires.

That may sound like harsh language for describing the relationship between the lovely Duchess and her gentle Antonio, but the diction, as well as the shape, of the scenes clearly points to a similarity in quality. When Ferdinand offers him gold, Bosola immediately assumes that Ferdinand is trying, as his brother had done, to hire an assassin. His strange ethics render him more offended when Ferdinand explains his actual intention:[10]

> I give you that
> To live i'th' court, here; and observe the duchess,
> To note all the particulars of her 'haviour;
> What suitors do solicit her for marriage
> And whom she best affects: she's a young widow—
> I would not have her marry again.

> (1. 1. 251–56)

Bosola responds: "It seems you would create me / One of your familiars" and goes on to define this term as "a very quaint invisible *devil,* in flesh: / An intelligencer." When Ferdinand admits that this is true and suggests that "ere long, *thou mayst arrive* / At a *higher place* by 't [my emphases]," Bosola rejects him, rather self-righteously for a convicted murderer:

> Take your *devils* [my emphasis]
> Which hell calls angels: these curs'd gifts would make
> You a corrupter, me an impudent traitor,
> And should I take these they'd take me to hell.

> (1. 1. 258–66)

Surely, it is no accident that Webster should choose similar diction at the moment when Antonio realizes which way the Duchess's thoughts are tending:

> *Ant.* There is a saucy, and ambitious *devil*
> Is dancing in this circle.

10. See David Luisi, "The Function of Bosola in *The Duchess of Malfi,*" p. 511.

Duch.   Remove him.
Ant.   How?
Duch. There needs small conjuration, when your finger
         May do it: thus—is it fit?
         [*She puts her ring on his finger:*] *he kneels.*
Ant.   What said you?
Duch.   Sir,
         This goodly roof of yours is too low built,
         I cannot stand upright in't, nor discourse,
         Without I raise it higher: raise yourself [my emphases],
         Or if you please, my hand to help you: so. [*Raises him.*]
                                          (1. 1. 412–19)

At one point, both Antonio and Bosola see themselves
tempted to or by something at least metaphorically infernal,
and both Ferdinand and the Duchess promise or effect a "rais-
ing" of their subjects for acquiescence to their wishes. It might
be argued that the analogy of action and diction in these two
scenes is used by Webster for contrast rather than evaluative
comparison, that the difference in quality of the people involved is brought out, by relief, through the similarity of forms.
But it seems to me that this is not the case because there are a
number of ways in which Webster prepares for and reinforces
the negative judgment implied here upon the behavior of Antonio and the Duchess. The incident that separates the two
"wooing" scenes is one of his means of preparing for that judgment.

Although this scene separates them temporally, its matter—
her brothers' admonitions against the Duchess's remarrying—
strengthens the link between the two scenes rather than weak-
ens it. For example, the fullest ironies of Ferdinand's counsel
can, obviously, only be realized in light of the scene of Bosola's
corruption, and the implications of the Duchess's actions in the
following scene can only be measured in light of those ironies.
Ferdinand's remarks to her are, of course, the height of hypocrisy, and yet they contain a true, if not an honest, warning—
for the audience as well as the Duchess:

    Hypocrisy is woven of a fine small thread,
    Subtler than Vulcan's engine: yet, believe't,
    Your darkest actions—nay, your privat'st thoughts—
    Will come to light.
                                          (1. 1. 313–16)

Hypocrisy is indeed woven of a fine, small thread, subtler than Vulcan's engine. Ferdinand should know—he has just been weaving such an "engine" in which he will eventually catch the Duchess and Antonio as surely as Vulcan caught Venus and Mars (and with far more disastrous results for all concerned). He can confidently warn her that her thoughts and actions are subject to exposure if she practices hypocrisy because he has already spread the net. The Duchess, of course, does not share the audience's insight into her brother's remarks, so, all around, we seem to have here a classic instance of dramatic irony.

Indeed, dramatic irony abounds in both brothers' admonitions. All that they say to her has been or will be borne out by the play. We have seen that the court is a "rank pasture"; the Duchess's "fame" really will be poisoned; her "marriage night" does turn out to be the "entrance into some prison," a prison of secrecy, constraint, and, finally, torment, and death. When Ferdinand describes the attitude that would enable her to make a secret marriage as "like the irregular crab, / Which though't goes backward, thinks it goes right, / Because it goes its own way" (1. 1. 319–21), the play bears out his perception of her willfulness in the speech that follows his exit. The Duchess asks, "Shall this move me?" and answers herself, "If all my royal kindred / Lay in my way unto this marriage, / I'd make them my low footsteps" (1. 1. 341–43). She betrays the state of mind he prophetically attributed to her even more succinctly in her remark that she is "going into a wilderness, / Where I shall find nor path, nor friendly clew / To be my guide" (1. 1. 359–61). That her actions will lead her away from the power, prerogatives, privileges, and security that her rank and the political order secure for her gives dramatic, ironic weight to her choice of the word *wilderness*.[11] In short, the play provides both immediate and ultimate confirmation of her brothers' judgments and predictions and seems, thus, to be incorporating their perspective on the Duchess in its treatment of her.

Obviously, the paradox in this scene goes beyond dramatic irony—as we usually think of it. Here, we have the villains of the piece presenting what is apparently authorial comment on the action, and it seems to me that this paradoxical technique has been partly responsible for leading many critics astray from

11. See James L. Calderwood, "*The Duchess of Malfi*: Styles of Ceremony," p. 147, and Eloise K. Goreau, *Integrity of Life: Allegorical Imagery in the Plays of John Webster*, p. 80.

the paths of Websterian virtue. Webster took a great risk in giving them the play's voice at this point.[12] The audience may be so put off by the quality of the speakers that it will miss the validity of their judgment on the Duchess's actions. Yet, Webster accomplishes at least two things by thus muting his judgment of her so early in the play. On the one hand, he keeps himself above reproach ethically by offering this perspective to the audience. On the other hand, he keeps the audience's sympathy for Antonio and the Duchess, thus inviting the complicity that is essential to his complex rhetorical structure and that is also characteristic of the genre. As I said in Chapter 2, this complicity in a behavior that leads to chaos convinces us of the value of those institutions that men have erected against the evil potential in all of us.

We cannot legitimately accuse Webster of deception because immediately before the brothers begin their remarks, he provides us with a rhetorical cue that ought to prepare us for the paradox to come. Bosola's last comment before this scene is, "Sometimes the devil doth preach" (1. 1. 291). That is a fair description of what we get in the brothers' counsel. The devil may quote Scripture for his own ends, but that speaker and those ends do not invalidate Scripture. That, it seems to me, is the logic of Webster's use of Ferdinand and the Cardinal as spokesmen. Although right for the wrong reasons, in light of the results of the Duchess's actions, they truly express the play's perspective at this point.

It is important to recognize that Antonio's capitulation to the Duchess in the next scene does constitute a fall and to understand the implications of that fall, because the effect of the action upon him is one of the gauges of value throughout the play. As we have seen, Antonio begins as a model of political, ethical probity, one who not only professes ideals but also believes they may be put into effect. In his eyes, the court of a prince may be the fountain of good governance he has seen the French king attempting to establish. Princes may enact laws, enforce justice, and provide their subjects with the example of

12. For a discussion illuminating my sense of the voice of a play, see Edgar T. Schell, "Who Said That—Hamlet or *Hamlet?*" Hirsch also makes a comment which addresses this question: "In a play . . . the total meaning of an utterance is not the intentional object of the dramatic character: that meaning is simply a component in the more complex intention of the dramatist. The speaker himself is spoken," p. 243.

behavior that, when they emulate it, will ensure order, virtue, and harmony in the land. Yet, by the end of the play, he will insist that his son fly the courts of princes, convinced by his experience with the Duchess and her brothers that his ideals are not viable in the face of reality, that, in his words, "the great are like the base."

It is equally important to recognize the Duchess's culpability in this fall and her responsibility for the events that destroy this idealism and, ultimately, this man she loves. Because her brothers are also rulers, because their machinations dominate the first half of Act 1, and because the Duchess is hardly seen or heard until their departure, it has been easy to apply the standards explicit in Antonio's speech and implicit in the actions, images, and dialogue I have been discussing only to them. Perhaps that is why so many critics have ignored her role as ruler or, at least, the applicability of those standards to her. Yet, as I said before, this is her court; this is where the action will take place. When her brothers leave and take their rotten retinue with them, it is only to her and her court that those standards may apply. Hers is the responsibility for creating a "fix'd" order and providing good example; hers is the will that must be subordinated to the common weal. At their departure, the generic expectation is that in the action to follow she will prove equal or unequal to that responsibility.

After her brothers' departure and before Antonio's entrance, the Duchess is left alone on the stage with Cariola, her waiting-woman. We have been made fully aware of the danger of her situation and her willfulness in persisting in the intention to marry. Now, if ever, she needs someone to counsel her, to point out what she ought to foresee. But her woman is the only one present, and she is both socially and characteristically unlikely to offer such counsel. Besides, she has been bound to secrecy and is thus already culpably involved:

> *Duch.* To thy known secrecy I have given up
> More than my life, my fame:—
> *Cari.*   Both shall be safe:
> For I'll conceal this secret from the world
> As warily as those that trade in poison
> Keep poison from their children.
> *Duch.*   Thy protestation
> Is ingenious and hearty: I believe it.
>
> (1. 1. 350–55)

If I were directing *The Duchess of Malfi*, I would have the Duchess deliver that last line somewhat wryly. Cariola could scarcely have lit on an unhappier or less reassuring analogy. In comparing the secret (marriage) to poison, she may be "ingenuous," but Webster certainly is not.[13] Once again he is using the image of poison as rhetorical metonymy, recalling the opening trope that established the ethical, political standards of the play and that serves as metaphor of the play's action. By equating the marriage to poison, Cariola truly, though unwittingly, prophesies the consequences and implies the negative aspects of the Duchess's intentions. She and Cariola, and soon Antonio, are, indeed, trading in poison. This marriage will cause the Duchess to lose the "fame" she values more than life and to provide the curs'd example that will demoralize her court, cause the confiscation of her duchy, result in her imprisonment and death, and destroy all that she loves.

A final irony of Cariola's "ingenious" protestation underlines the Duchess's folly in believing she may defy political ideals and realities in order to find happiness as a woman: Her persistence in making the secret and unequal marriage guarantees that she will not be able to keep the poison she is trading in from her own children. Because of the conditions of this marriage, they are doomed before they are even conceived. Thus, by means of this image Webster sounds a warning and makes a judgment despite the complicity to which we are invited by the charm, wit, and grace of the Duchess's wooing of Antonio.

Obviously, this scene has all those elements, and just as obviously Webster is using them to invite that sympathetic response that will divert our attention from the immediate judgment invoked by the image and action. We suspect from Antonio's glowing description of the Duchess (1. 1. 187–204) that he is more than half in love with her already, and there is a certain delight in being in on the secret that their love is reciprocal before either of the lovers is aware of it. We can take a benign pleasure in their mutual insecurity. Yet, lest we should come at the end to accuse Webster of totally obscuring the nature of their actions, of weighting the rhetorical scales

13. See John Russell Brown's note, *The Duchess of Malfi*, p. 29, on "ingenious." He glosses it as intelligent, sagacious, "but the word was often used for 'ingenuous,' and this sense may also be required here." Other editors, for example, John Addington Symonds, in *John Webster and Cyril Tourneur: Four Plays*, p. 137, gloss it only as "ingenuous." That seems to me more in keeping with Webster's irony.

against us, he provides a second negative comment through Cariola.

After Antonio has led the Duchess off to their nuptial bed, Cariola muses: "Whether the spirit of greatness or of woman / Reign most in her, I know not, but it shows / A fearful madness; I owe her much of pity" (1. 1. 504–6). Cariola's judgment is that the spirit manifested in the Duchess's action shows madness— although she cannot decide whether that spirit is of her "greatness" or of her sex. In other words, what has overpowered her reason, the willfulness developed in her because of her rank or the passion of the woman for Antonio? Perhaps it is both. In any case, Cariola and, I think, the play conclude that regardless of which has sway, there is madness here. Certainly, the image of poison just discussed implies this, and the consequences of her action bear this out. And unless we are to assume, as many have, that a cosmic cynicism is at work here that punishes the guiltless (or the only venially guilty) with horrendous torments for slight indiscretions, I think we must look at the madness manifested in her marriage in light of the dialectic established by Cariola's remark.[14]

The primary importance of this remark is its insistence on the Duchess's rank—despite the personal, sentimental charm of her marriage rites with Antonio. The crux of the Duchess's problem in this marriage is that while she has both power and responsibility, she also has the traditional limitations of her sex. The status of a woman in marriage was one of dependency on and deference to her husband—in accordance with the Pauline analogy between the marriage relationship and the relationship between Christ and the Church. The noblewoman, no matter how powerful her connections or how high her rank, was traditionally reduced to secondary status in marriage, assuming whatever title, position, and privilege her husband could bestow on her and relinquishing any deference or power to which her former high rank might entitle her. This was such a commonplace that James used it, rather whimsically, as an excuse to bestow an earldom on his favorite, Robert Carr, before the latter's wedding to Frances Howard: "Expressing a kindly wish not to see the lady reduced from a countess to a mere viscount-

14. On this question of the dialectic revealed in Cariola's remark, compare Calderwood, *The Duchess of Malfi*, p. 142; Lagarde, *John Webster*, 2:848; Travis Bogard, *The Tragic Satire of John Webster*, p. 65; Leonora Leet Brodwin, *Elizabethan Love Tragedy, 1587–1625*, p. 284.

ess, King James . . . obligingly advanced Carr to the dignity of Earl of Somerset."[15]

It might be argued that the Duchess's situation was different, more nearly analogous to that of a queen than of a countess and that this would make her an exception to these "rules." Certainly, the duchies of fifteenth-century Italy were more like independent kingdoms than were those of sixteenth- or seventeenth-century England. Yet, they owed fealty of different sorts to both emperor and pope. In ambiguous situations, possession of a duchy apparently depended on who got to pope or emperor first. That Webster assumed this political situation is borne out in the conversation between the two pilgrims at the shrine at Ancona, who function in this play as the vox populi figures discussed in Chapter 2:[16]

1st. Pil.	Here's a strange turn of state! who would have thought	
	So great a lady would have match'd herself	
	Unto so mean a person? yet the cardinal	
	Bears himself much too cruel.	
2nd. Pil.		They are banished.
1st. Pil.	But I would ask what power this state	
	Of Ancona to determine of a free prince?	
2nd. Pil.	They are a free state sir, and her brother show'd	
	How that the Pope, fore-hearing of her looseness,	
	Hath seiz'd into th' protection of the church	
	The dukedom, which she held as dowager.	
1st. Pil.	But by what justice?	
2nd. Pil.		Sure, I think by none,
	Only her brother's instigation.	

(3. 4. 24–35)

This exchange also bears out that being a ruler did not exempt a woman from those marriage-related problems that plagued other noblewomen. Remembering the problems of Mary Tudor and Mary Stuart, Jacobeans would probably have felt that it merely compounded them. Like Mary Stuart, the Duchess ruled as an independent prince, equal in status to her brothers, but, in actuality, her sex put her in a very precarious position as ruler. In Act 1 Webster gives us forceful and graphic evidence of the intrigue, the power struggle, in which her brothers are going to involve her. In line with the discussion of

15. G. P. V. Akrigg, *Jacobean Pageant or the Court of King James I,* p. 186.
16. See Lagarde, *John Webster,* 2:845, and 2:901. He comes down quite hard on the Duchess for remarriage and for mesalliance.

queens' marriages in Chapter 2, it seems to me that the most obvious reason why they want to keep her from remarrying would be that as long as she remains a widow, she is, theoretically, ruler of self and duchy as well. But given the traditional role of women in marriage, if she remarries, she will accept, at least privately, the rule of her husband.[17] Should she marry an equal or greater prince, Ferdinand and the Cardinal would lose any possibility of controlling her actions, either as sister or as Duchess. That would seem to be the logic, if we may take him seriously, of Ferdinand's suggesting the controllable Malateste as a husband for the Duchess. It is certainly reminiscent of the Earl of Moray's resistance to both of the Scottish marriages of his half-sister Mary, for during the times when she was unattached and reconciled with him, Mary repeatedly showed a tendency to be controlled by his counsel and moral support.[18]

Certainly, the desire to control or ultimately obtain the wealth of her duchy was the shield that Ferdinand used to keep himself from facing any darker reasons against her remarriage, according to his own words after her death:

> What was the meanness of her match to me?
> Only I must confess, I had a hope,
> Had she continu'd widow, to have gain'd
> An infinite mass of treasure by her death:
> And that was the main cause.

> (4. 2. 282–86)

We may or may not accept that this was the cause, but we must accept that it was, at some point, present in Ferdinand's mind as a sort of politically "acceptable" motivation.

Much of this may seem highly conjectural, but as I said earlier, Antonio has no more power with which to counter her brothers' machinations than she can bestow on him. As the pilgrims' exchange reveals, by marrying him, especially in a secret marriage, the consequences of which will give her a public reputation for looseness, she provides her brothers with the means for depriving her of her duchy. This seizure of her duchy

17. As Carroll Camden notes in discussing the "place" of women in marriage, the family was considered a microcosm of the body politic. "In this commonwealth, it is the husband's office to give the proper orders." *The Elizabethan Woman*, p. 110.

18. Maurice Lee, Jr., *James Stewart, Earl of Moray: A Political Study of the Reformation in Scotland*, pp. 76–87, 90, 97, 104.

and the Pope's censure of her looseness would assuredly have recalled Mary Queen of Scots' difficulties, which I mentioned in Chapter 2. Mary's subjects, the Pope, and her Continental Catholic allies all turned from her because of her loss of reputation over Darnley's murder and the Bothwell marriage that followed.[19] Thus, her lords could force her to abdicate in favor of her infant son James and imprison her at Lochleven with no danger of retribution. Obviously, the analogy to Mary's situation indicates that for Webster's audience, being a queen or a sovereign duchess did not permit a woman to disregard her traditional vulnerability when contracting a marriage.

How different the Duchess's situation might have been, from the Jacobean standpoint, had she remained only the widow of the Duke of Malfi instead of secretly marrying a man beneath her in rank, and thereby getting that reputation for looseness, is implied in the celebrated case of the Countess Dowager of Rutland. In 1605, several merchants and artisans of London had her arrested for debt when she failed to pay their bills. This led to a debate in the Star Chamber over how far noblemen and women were liable to arrest, considering the privilege of their rank.[20] More specifically, it was asked what the privilege of wives and widows of noblemen were. The verdict went against the countess's creditors, and the conclusion, which has a striking bearing on the Duchess's predicament, was that "they have the like privileges as their husbands, unless they marry ignobly or live dishonourably."[21] Thus, this marriage, grown out of the Duchess's private desires as woman, is at direct odds with her "greatness," that is, her rank and responsibility.

It seems to me that this is the basis on which Webster primarily condemns the Duchess's second marriage—not because of any merely social or strictly religious norms, the terms in which it has most often been discussed. Of course, it is true that second marriages were officially disapproved by the Church and Webster himself implies disapproval of remarriage in the contrast between the *Characters* attributed to him of "A Vertuous Widdow" and "An Ordinarie Widow" (see appendix). Fur-

---

19. See, for example, James Emerson Phillips, *Images of a Queen: Mary Stuart in Sixteenth Century Literature,* Chapter 3, pp. 52–84, on the effect that Mary's loss of reputation had on the Continent.

20. Akrigg, *Jacobean Pageant,* p. 229.

21. G. B. Harrison, *A Second Jacobean Journal: Being a Record of Those Things Most Talked of during the Years 1607 to 1610,* p. 238.

ther, as the judgment in the Countess Dowager's case implied
and Lady Arabella Stuart's fate proved, secret and/or unequal
marriages were also condemned for various social, economic,
and political reasons. Finally, these reasons, as well as the religious ones, cause disapproval of the Duchess's and Antonio's
marriage in Webster's sources. But, while these extrinsic con-
siderations of sanction, source, and topical concern provide illuminating supplementary evidence in discussing Webster's attitudes, the play itself continues to provide intrinsically the
scale of values against which the Duchess's actions can be measured.

Critics have seen Ferdinand's speech on Reputation, in Act 3,
Scene 2, as just another of those points at which Webster is
unable to resist a sententious, and inapposite, excursion. Yet,
hearkening back to Antonio's opening speech, we must be reminded that, as would be expected in commonweal tragedy, the
loss of reputation that is so personally and politically disastrous
for the Duchess has an ethical dimension that goes beyond her
own fate. In terms of the genre's set on the world, it is also more
damning. Regardless of how her private motives and justifications extenuate her actions on the personal level, her public
behavior provides the curs'd example that, Antonio's image
insists, poisons the common fountain of government at its
source. Webster's focus upon this generic assumption is especially pointed in the context of a country demoralized by the
example of James's court.

Ironically, James himself had expressed the political doctrine
that denies absolution to the Duchess on the basis of any private virtue: "For it is not ynough that ye haue and reteyne (as
prisoners) with in your selfe neuer so many good qualities and
vertues, except yee employe them and set them on worke for
the weall of them that are committed to your charge."[22] In
terms that are remarkably appropriate to the Duchess, he goes
on to explain the consequences of a private virtue that, nevertheless, looks publicly like vice:

> It is a true old saying, that a king is as one set on a skaffold, whose
> smallest actions and gestures al the people gazingly do behold:
> and therefore although a king be neuer so precise in the discharg-
> ing of his office, the people who seeth byt the outwarde parte, will
> euer judge of the substance by the circumstances, & according to

22. James I, *Basilikon Doron,* p. 73.

the outwarde appearance (if his behauiour be light or dissolute)
will conceiue preoccupied conceits of the King's inwarde intentions; which although with time (the tryer of all trueth) it wil
vanish, yet *interum patitur iustus:* and prejudged conceites will (in
the meane time) breed contempt, the Mother of Rebellion and
disorder.[23]

Any attempt to excuse her pursuit of a course that violates
her responsibility on the grounds that she is ignorant of its
implications is undercut by the play. Her words immediately
after her brothers' departure and before her wooing of Antonio
indicate that she is well aware of the conflict between her public
role and her private desires. She speaks of "going into a wilderness," of the "misery of us that are born great"; and as Calderwood implies, the rhetorical strategies she employs reveal how
clearly she recognizes that her roles as duchess and and as
woman are at odds in the situation.[24] Being a duchess forces her
to violate the decorum of courtship and act the "man's role."
Being a woman forces her to violate the decorum of rank by
suing where she might otherwise command. As she says:

> The misery of us that are born great—
> We are forc'd to woo, because none dare woo us:
> And as a tyrant doubles with his words,
> And fearfully equivocates, so we
> Are forc'd to express our violent passions
> In riddles, and in dreams, and leave the path
> Of simple virtue, which was never made
> To seem the thing it is not.
>
> (1. 1. 441–48)

She is, however, willing to pursue this course and, in her
secret marriage, to place her desire for Antonio above decorum,
"simple virtue," legality, and political responsibility. Her willingness to place her private imperatives above the imperatives
of rule identifies her with her brothers, and, as we have seen,
the play has already judged them negatively on that score.

Perhaps it seems perverse to lump the Duchess with her
brothers. From the moment of Antonio's description of her, we
are invited to see her as different from them in everything but
rank. For rhetorical purposes, Webster wants us to approve of
the Duchess and to condemn her brothers even more for the

---

23. Ibid., pp. 121–22.
24. See Calderwood, *The Duchess of Malfi,* p. 137.

apparent contrast she offers to them. Until the point at which Antonio capitulates to her desires, his judgments not only give him a good character, but the corroboration of those judgments seems to make him a spokesman for the play's values. Thus, by having Antonio follow his negative description of her brothers with a glowing description of the Duchess, Webster is going out of his way to engage our sympathies for her. We still expect Antonio's description to be just, and further, we value her because she is valued by him:[25]

> But for their sister, the right noble duchess—
> You never fix'd your eye on three fair medals,
> Cast in one figure, of so different temper:
> For her discourse, it is so full of rapture
> You only will begin then to be sorry
> When she doth end her speech; and wish, in wonder,
> She held it less vain-glory to talk much,
> Than you penance to hear her: whilst she speaks,
> She throws upon a man so sweet a look,
> That it were able to raise one to a galliard
> That lay in a dead palsy, and to dote
> On that sweet countenance: but in that look,
> There speaketh so divine a continence
> As cuts off all lascivious, and vain hope.
> Her days are practis'd in such noble virtue
> That sure her nights—nay more, her very sleeps—
> Are more in heaven than other ladies' shrifts.
> Let all sweet ladies break their flatt'ring glasses,
> And dress themselves in her.

(1. 1. 187–205)

Even while Antonio is emphasizing the differences between the Duchess and her brothers, Webster is insisting on one similarity. Obviously, there is a strong physical resemblance among these "three fair medals, / Cast in one figure." This resemblance is, surely, no more a random element in the play than the qualitative twinship of Ferdinand and the Cardinal or the actual twinship of Ferdinand and the Duchess. It has been argued that the physical bond between the latter two is used

25. This speech contains a number of echoes of the character of "A Vertuous Widdow." Considering that the Duchess turns out not to have the qualities attributed to her, nor to remain a widow, virtuous or otherwise, Webster would seem to be echoing those lines ironically (which might be a good argument for dating the Characters earlier or *The Duchess* later than has been done). See appendix.

only to make their spiritual difference more striking.[26] But I do not think that is the case.

Fittingly, the first indication of Antonio's fallibility and the first of his judgments to be denied by the play concerns the Duchess's psychic continence. If it is true that her days "are practis'd in such noble virtue," and her nights and very sleeps "are more in heaven, than other ladies' shrifts," one wonders during what hours she conceived such a passion for Antonio. As Lagarde puts it, "the flattering picture that Antonio paints does not coincide exactly with reality: the thoughts of the Duchess are less chaste than he asserts and a little closer to what Ferdinand imagines."[27]

The first speech she delivers when she and Cariola finally have the stage alone is a contradiction of almost all his claims about her "continence" and her temperament in general. Antonio has apparently been so dazzled by externals and by her public comportment that he has no notion of the intensity of emotion and the obduracy of will in this woman. And the former is a quality she shares with Ferdinand, the latter with both her brothers.

Not only is the lovely Duchess like her brothers in placing private desire above public responsibility, but, ironically, she goes them one worse by taking the laws of both State and Church into her own hands in order to realize that desire. She dispenses with the laws of State thus: "I have heard lawyers say, a contract in a chamber / *Per verba de presenti* is absolute marriage" (1. 1. 478–79). Then she dictates her terms to the Church: "How can the church bind faster? / We now are man and wife, and 'tis the church / That must but echo this" (1. 1. 491–93).[28] The assumption that she can invert "all good lawes

26. Alexander Allison, "Ethical Themes in *The Duchess of Malfi*," p. 267. For an interesting discussion of the apparent irrelevance of this resemblance, see Potter, "Realism Versus Nightmare," pp. 183–84.

27. Lagarde, *John Webster*, 2:84, my translation. See also Brodwin, *Elizabethan Love Tragedy*, p. 287; Goreau, *Integrity of Life*, p. 165; Ralph Berry, *The Art of John Webster*, pp. 53–54. In Painter's account, of course, the contention that the Duchess's "nights are more in heaven than other ladies' shrifts" is flatly denied. Painter goes on at some length describing the Duchess's nightly erotic fantasies, her suffering, and, finally, her settling on Antonio as the most likely individual around.

28. For a discussion of such private ceremonies see Camden, *The Elizabethan Woman*, p. 85ff. Politically, the most important question here is the legitimacy of the issue of marriages contracted in this manner. In seeing the Duchess's children as bastards Ferdinand is taking the Catholic position of the Councils

to serue only [her] unrulie private affections" is reminiscent of James's description of the tyrant, quoted in Chapter 2.

Her passion for Antonio is certainly more appealing and less reprehensible than the viciousness and malevolence that motivate her brothers, but she is no more a private person than they, and her actions can never affect only her own fate. Her desire to marry Antonio may seem innocent, even laudable, to us, but given the assumptions of the genre, when she turns her eyes inward to personal happiness and her back upon her responsibility as ruler, she creates the conditions in which power will be separated from justice. She will be the first to feel the hand of an injustice that is yet the manifestation of a higher justice. Thus, although Bosola will later say that the Cardinal took from Justice her most equal balance when he killed his sister, it is actually she who initially upset the balance in opting for personal satisfaction despite the obvious and impinging political realities of her situation.

Further, a Jacobean audience wearily accustomed to a king who repeatedly placed his personal gratifications above the necessities of rule would not, I think, react as indulgently toward the Duchess as we do. Orthodox political theory had long insisted that rulers might not see personal felicity as owed to them: "Let them thynke the greater dominion they have, that therby they sustayne the more care and studie. And that therfore they must have the lasse solace and passetyme, and to sensuall pleasures lasse opportunitie."[29]

The Duchess's insistence that "all discord, without this circumference, / Is only to be pitied, and not fear'd" perhaps reveals that she is more politically naive than cavalier. Nevertheless, the juxtaposition of her rank, her departure from "the path of simple virtue" into deception, her own and Antonio's awareness that the impropriety of their marriage requires this deception, and the quality of her brothers and of her court make it clear that her action is folly on the personal level and irresponsibility on the public level. It seems to me that Webster had

---

of Trent and Lateran (ibid., pp. 92–93) that decreed clandestine marriages void and their issue illegitimate. The Duchess, in seeing her marriage primarily as a contract, is taking a more Protestant view (ibid., p. 84). Once again, Arabella Stuart is pertinent: The fact of her being married, secretly, did not change James's attitude or his power to imprison her—anymore than it changed Ferdinand's.

29. Sir Thomas Elyot, *The Book of the Governour*, p. 118.

pointed to this, searingly, in the irony of Antonio's summation of the Duchess's virtues: "All her particular worth grows to this sum: / She stains the time past, lights the time to come" (1. 1. 208–9). All of the suffering, murder, and madness that fill "the time to come" in the play can be traced back to her abdication of responsibility as surely as the same sorts of consequences in *King Lear* can be traced back to Lear's actual abdication.

A further and more negative irony might have been apparent to Webster's audience in his use of these lines. The second of them is virtually a quotation from "A Monumental Column" in which Webster apostrophizes Henry as young Mecaenas, "Whose beames shall break forth from thy hollow Tombe / Staine the time past, and light the time to come!"[30] Since his eulogy of Prince Henry was written during the time Webster was composing *The Duchess of Malfi*, his use of the line could hardly be unconscious recall. Nor, I think, could we accept it as a thrift that implies poverty of invention. As my discussion of him in Chapter 2 implies, Henry's "light" was the ideal of princely behavior he embodied. The Duchess can hardly be said to have embodied that ideal in Act 1. Thus, Webster's use of the line would seem to be yet another ironic way of implying those standards of judgment against which her claim that she can both live and die like a prince must be measured.

By the end of Act 1, those standards have been established and the action that violates them set in motion. Implicitly, Antonio's opening metaphor of the action is syllogistic: If the common fountain of the prince's court from which good governance should flow is poisoned by curs'd example, then the consequences, "death and diseases," will spread outward until they encompass the whole land. It remains to be seen how the remainder of the play completes the syllogism.

30. John Webster, "A Monumental Column," p. 282, ll. 277–78; Lucas, *The Complete Works of John Webster*, 3:268–92.

4

The Poisoned Fountain

Act 2 will reveal the most immediate consequences of the Duchess's "madness" in marrying Antonio. Given the affective relationship between ruler and ruled which informs the genre, it is to be expected that her disordered choice will bring about disorder in her duchy. In placing her "good" above political Good, she has loosed a force of misrule that turns expectations into their opposites and foils the innocent and guilty alike. Many of the play's detractors have seen the workings of this force in the play and, quite understandably, identified them as flaws in structural logic or verisimilitude. But, given what he is trying to represent, it seems to me that Webster's logic is defensible and that there is a kind of stark probability in the play. I do not mean to argue from imitative form, but the attempt to represent disorder strains, obviously, against the very nature of art, and Webster's job is to represent that force through its effects. Opening Act 2 to the sound of Bosola's voice is an economical and effective way to begin.

Here we have the kind of man who should be purged from a wholesome country, according to Antonio's speech. Instead, he has been made a privileged member of the Duchess's court. Lest we think the "provisorship of the horse" a mean office, it should be remembered that Elizabeth's favorite, the Earl of Leicester, enjoyed this post in her court.[1] Part of Bosola's "privilege" is the indulgence virtually everyone shows his coarse manner and blunt speech. By allowing Bosola to open Act 2 with a cynical catechism of Castruchio on the ways of becoming "an eminent courtier," followed by a disgusting satire against the vanity of court ladies, Webster accomplishes several things. He implies that the Duchess is no more concerned than King James with setting standards or maintaining discipline; he provides us with a picture of the expedient realities of court life, as opposed to the normative ideals; and he effectively taints the atmosphere in which we next see Antonio and the Duchess.

In the context of a speech claiming that man is even less worthy than the animals, Bosola is allowed to discover to the

1. Fernand Lagarde, *John Webster,* 1:442.

audience the first consequence of the Duchess's actions. Apparently she is pregnant, and the terms in which Bosola introduces this news graphically emphasize the unpleasant physical aspects of pregnancy rather than any ideal spiritual (or sentimental) aspects of motherhood:

> I observe our duchess
> Is sick o' days, she pukes, her stomach seethes,
> The fins of her eyelids look most teeming blue,
> She wanes i'th' cheek, and waxes fat i'th' flank;
> And (contrary to our Italian fashion)
> Wears a loose-body'd gown—there's somewhat in't!
>
> (2. 1. 63–68)

Of course, it can be argued that Bosola's conventional role of malcontent, his melancholic temper, and his dirty mind render his view of her pregnancy an unreliable guide to Webster's. Yet, in Act 2, Scene 2, the juxtaposing of Bosola's speeches and the Duchess's speeches and actions implies that despite the excess and the distortion of Bosola's expression, his perspective is not wholly false.[2]

Immediately on the heels of Bosola's speech, Antonio enters, confiding the secret of the marriage to Delio. There is something rather ludicrous in hearing someone sworn to secrecy over a matter the effect of which grows more apparent by the day. Surely, if Bosola has noticed the Duchess's condition, it can hardly have gone unnoticed by others. Her rank may enable her to put aside the laws of Church and State, but it cannot enable her to put aside the laws of nature nor to blind those around her to her condition. When a duchess yields to her sexual passion, she is as liable to the consequences as the lowliest milkmaid, and Bosola takes up the question of this leveling power of passion immediately.

He enters into a discussion with Antonio of their relative responses to preferment, which culminates in this statement:

> Some would think the souls of princes were brought forth by some more weighty cause than those of meaner persons—they are deceived, there's the same hand to them: the like passions sway them, the same reason that makes a vicar go to law for a tithe-pig and undo his neighbors, makes them spoil a whole province, and batter down goodly cities with the cannon.
>
> (2. 1. 101–7)

2. Ibid., 2:915.

As many Jacobeans apparently did, Bosola takes it for granted that princes can be expected to place private desire over public responsibility—and for passions just like those that sway "meaner persons." With that, the Duchess enters, in full flower, as it were, and displays all the stereotypical tetchiness, hysteria, and voraciousness attributed to pregnant women of whatever rank. As if to confirm Bosola's observations further, she proceeds to give evidence that her particular passion will cause her, if not to batter down goodly cities, at least to attempt to batter down distinctions of degree. In order that her husband should not have to demean himself before her in public, she asks him if she has not heard him say "that the French courtiers / Wear their hats on 'fore the king" and why she should not "bring up that fashion." After all, she says, " 'Tis ceremony more than duty, that consists / In the removing of a piece of felt: / Be you the example to the rest o' th' court, / Put on your hat first" (2. 1. 118–24). Antonio demurs and his demurrer recalls what she has forgotten—that proper ceremony is not demeaning: "You must pardon me: / I have seen, in colder countries than in France, / Nobles stand bare to th' prince; and the distinction / Methought show'd reverently" (2. 1. 125–28). In other words, Antonio sees the practice she invites him to as a negative one, disruptive to good governance. Unlike some of James's courtiers, Antonio will not act the part of the royal favorite who presumes on the prince's affections to subvert his dignity.

It might be argued that I take too seriously what is merely a bit of domestic play on the Duchess's part. However, I think my reading of the significant juxtaposition of Bosola's comments and her actions would be supported for Jacobeans, at any rate, by another of those striking similarities to the history of Mary Stuart. Watching Mary, as always, for evidence of instability and weakness that might be to Elizabeth's advantage, an Englishman at the Scottish queen's court after her ill-advised marriage to Bothwell reported the following to Cecil: "The Duke openly uses great reverence to the Queen, ordinarily bareheaded, which she seems she would have otherwise, and will sometimes take his cap and put it on."[3] Cecil's correspondent would hardly have been presenting this as a bit of charming badinage intended to win sympathy for Mary. A queen might forgive presumption but she should not encourage it.

3. Frank Arthur Mumby, *The Fall of Mary Stuart: A Narrative in Contemporary Letters*, p. 243.

There is a distinction, however, between Mary's and the Duchess's situation that is in Mary's favor. Those present when she placed the cap on Bothwell's head knew why she did so. He was, after all, her husband, and it is unlikely that they would have presumed upon his example. The Duchess's courtiers, on the other hand, do not know of her relationship with Antonio and are expressly invited to see him as "the example to the rest o' th' court."

In refusing to provide that example, Antonio seems to be restored to the role of normative spokesman that he held at the beginning. He is acting as a proper counsellor, but, of course, in doing so, he is not acting as a proper husband. Clearly, the Duchess cannot have it both ways: Her husband cannot be subject and still be head of the household, at least not publicly. Her desire to have the prerogatives of a private person is not going to stop at the bedroom door. At this point, she is trying to give up one of the prerogatives of her rank, voluntarily. Ironically, it will become apparent that she has created circumstances that will ultimately deprive her, step by step, of all her privileges, all her prerogatives, and all her power.

Although the Duchess and Antonio drop the question of the ruler-subject relationship when Bosola offers her his gift of apricots, Webster keeps it before us by means of his rhetorical metonymy. Antonio had claimed that if "curs'd example" poisoned the fountain of rule, the poison would spread throughout the land; obviously, the spread has begun. As a result of her actions, in addition to the apparent laxity of her court, the Duchess has made herself vulnerable to that "finely woven net" spread by Ferdinand, in the person of Bosola, who almost poisons her literally in his attempt to discover whether she is, indeed, pregnant. Webster (whose dramatic sense was surer than his physiology) has the Duchess greedily consume the fruit and then, as a result of its "greenness," or its having been ripened in horse dung, go into premature labor. One may be able to hide pregnancy behind those "bawd farthingales" and loose-bodied gowns, but labor is something else again. Immediately, the court is thrown into an uproar as the Duchess, Antonio, and those in their confidence are forced into lying, plotting, and arbitrary use of power in an attempt to cover up her condition. The diction Webster chooses for Delio's questions after the Duchess's hurried exit defines the atmosphere she has created in her court:[4] "Have you prepar'd / Those ladies to attend her? and *procur'd* / That *politic* safe conveyance for the midwife / Your duchess *plotted* [my emphases]?" (2. 1. 162–65).

The lewd joking of Bosola and the more explicitly lewd jesting of the officers about the Switzer "with a pistol in his great cod-piece" taken in the Duchess's bedchamber are hardly the sort of accompaniment to be expected for the lying-in of a duchess.[5] There is a quality of lese majesty in their developing conceit of pistol/pizzle, case/codpiece. The mock ingenuous "Who would have searched his cod-piece?" rejoined by "True, if he had kept out of the ladies' chambers" contains a suggestion that a fellow with a great codpiece is the sort of man that might be found in their Duchess's chamber, that what Bosola has observed has not been lost on them. The exchange implies that her officers no longer feel the awe accorded rank and have ceased to pay her the respect owed a duchess. In this they function subtly as vox populi figures and mark the degree to which curs'd example is beginning to disrupt her duchy.

That the story of the Switzer is immediately countered by a trumped up story of theft and that story, in turn, used to justify imprisoning everyone at court in his chamber overnight marks the spread of poisonous effect further. Because of the ambiguity of the Duchess's actions, hers has become a court in which order and decorum go by the board, where the private necessities of the ruler take precedence over ceremony and tradition. The leveling she seemed to desire begins in earnest and in various forms. Antonio's comment on their situation at the end of Scene 3 underlines these leveling consequences: *"The great are like the base—nay, they are the same— / When they seek shameful ways, to avoid shame"* (2. 3. 51–52).[6] Thus, her actions have not only had a physical effect upon the Duchess and a disordering effect upon her court, but they have brought about a moral leveling in Antonio as well. Once again, the effect of the action on him serves as a gauge of value. He and the Duchess have been forced by the necessities of her case to compromise their own quality

4. See P. F. Vernon, "The Duchess of Malfi's Guilt," p. 337.

5. Muriel West, *The Devil and John Webster,* p. 181. She speaks of the "matter of the servants' talk—part of a sustained connotative atmosphere of evil that surrounds the Duchess' lying-in."

6. See Vernon, "The Duchess of Malfi's Guilt," p. 337. He sees these lines as summing up the main theme of the play.

and, in so doing, have become the same as the "base." They are experiencing, and thus dramatizing, that generic truism, taken over from the moralities, that the vices we adopt to serve our ends inevitably master us.

In Scene 5, however, it becomes clear that her actions will have more serious consequences for her rule than a loss of credibility and a demoralized court. When Bosola's announcement of the birth of the Duchess's son reaches Ferdinand, his ranting reveals, implicitly, the affective relationship between her well-being and the common weal assumed by commonweal tragedy. The Cardinal asks him, "Why do you make yourself / So wild a tempest?" and Ferdinand rages:

> Would I could be one,
> That I might toss her palace 'bout her ears,
> Root up her goodly forests, blast her meads,
> And lay her general territory as waste
> As she hath done her honours.
>
> (2. 5. 17–21)

Could Ferdinand accomplish this, who would be the loser? Obviously, the Duchess would be the first victim, but the inhabitants of forest and mead would also be destroyed in the tempest, caught in a destructive fury aimed primarily at her. The battles that raged all over Scotland because of Mary's defiant marriage to Bothwell had exactly that effect. Ferdinand corroborates Bosola's contention—when swayed by passion the great will indeed spoil a whole province as readily as a "vicar will go to law for a tithe-pig, and undo his neighbors." Now, the effect of the Duchess's actions has spread beyond the court, the force she has loosed threatens to engulf all of those subjects whose well-being is her responsibility.

By the end of Act 2, the Duchess's desire to behave as a private person has jeopardized her country, her court, and herself—as duchess and as woman. She had wanted to put off certain troublesome aspects of her "greatness" that constricted her as woman, but the results of her actions reveal the indissoluble link between the power, prerogatives, and privileges on the one side and the responsibility of rule on the other that are assumed by the genre and political theory.[7] Her first abdication of responsibility, like Lear's, has set in motion a series of events

7. See Lagarde, *John Webster,* p. 839.

that strip her of power, take away her prerogatives, and deny her privileges. In secretly marrying a man her inferior in rank, she has created powerful enemies for herself and her people and, at the same time, effectively cut herself off from any hope of aid from outside her duchy.

In the beginning of Act 3 it becomes apparent that she has also cut herself off from support within. The ambiguity of her behavior has caused the "common rabble" to "directly say / She is a strumpet" (3. 1. 25–26), and Antonio's rise in power and wealth has become the object of envy among the courtiers. In pointing out these effects, Webster uses conventions very elliptically. Reporting these responses to Delio, Antonio provides evidence of the further effect of the Duchess's curs'd example and functions indirectly as a vox populi figure himself. We have already had implicit evidence of the effect of her behavior in the bawdy talk of her officers; thus, this "hearsay" reported by Antonio may be seen as valid and according to generic expectations.

As Act 2 deals with the subversion of order and decorum in the Duchess's court and implies her loss of reputation, Act 3 concerns itself with the consequences of that loss. She had counted on her position to secure her reputation ("let old women wink"), forgetting that her reputation might be needed to secure her position politically as well as socially. In Scene 1, following Antonio's report to Delio of the common rabble's opinion of her, the Duchess, perhaps in an attempt to sound her brother out, tells Ferdinand that "I am to have private conference with you / About a scandalous report, is spread / Touching mine honour" (3. 1. 46–48). Ferdinand protests that he wishes to be "ever deaf to't" and ironically counsels her to "be safe in your own innocency." When, later, he confronts her in her chamber in Scene 2, her first argument against him is that her reputation is safe. That jars strangely with her own earlier awareness of the scandalous report that concerned her honor.[8] Once again the Duchess seems to be attempting to force circumstances to conform to her perception of what is or what ought to be. Ferdinand tells her that she has "shook hands with Reputation, / And made him invisible" (3. 2. 134–35). That he voices the play's judgment on her is made clear in two ways. First, her own immediate course of action indicates that she

8. See R. W. Dent, _John Webster's Borrowings,_ p. 211.

feels that she has cause to fear loss of reputation and its consequences, and, second, as I said earlier, when her kingdom is
confiscated by the Pope, Webster makes clear that this second
loss is a result of the first.

The political effect that loss of princely reputation could have
was clearly manifested in Mary Stuart's relations with her people following the murder of Darnley, her second husband, and
her marriage to Bothwell. Her subjects often taunted her with
cries of "Adultress," "Whore," and "Strumpet" when she appeared among them. After her defeat at Carberry Hill, she was
openly confronted with banners that accused her pictorially of
complicity in Darnley's murder and of adultery with Bothwell,
both of which were substantiated for them by the haste and
circumstances of her marriage to the latter. As a result of the
disaffection of the Scots, her lords had no difficulty from them
when they deposed and imprisoned her.[9]

The Duchess responds to Ferdinand's discovery by making
up a lie, and, as Mary did, planning to flee from her duchy. In
deserting her province to the mercy of her enemies, she is, as
Leech has pointed out, behaving irresponsibly as a duchess in
order to secure herself as a private person.[10] Her behavior is
humanly but not politically understandable—ethically or
strategically. By remaining inside her duchy, she would force
her enemies to gather an army and invade the country to get at
her. Webster implies the improbability of such an invasion
through the martial situation he creates at this exact point in the
play. The emperor himself is involved in a war so weighty as
to be forced to "draft" a cardinal, who must resign his hat to
serve in the army again (3. 3. 1–8). At such a juncture, it seems
unlikely that there would be time or manpower to be spared for
a punitive expedition against the Duchess. Thus, her decision
to fly to Ancona is not only irresponsible but inept. However,
it is ironically fitting that she seems aware that there is some
relationship between her political security and her reputation
and that once her secret marriage is made known she will be in
trouble if she remains within her duchy. She reveals her aware-

9. George Malcolm Thomson, *The Crime of Mary Stuart*, pp. 122–26, and Chapters 11–12. See also Maurice Lee, Jr., *James Stewart, Earl of Moray: A Political Study
of the Reformation in Scotland*, p. 197.

10. Clifford Leech, *John Webster: A Critical Study*, pp. 64, 69. See also his *The
Duchess of Malfi*, p. 52. This is also, of course, the crux of his article, "An
Addendum to Webster's Duchess," pp. 253–56.

ness that "honour" and "safety" have some bearing upon one another and that her reputation is not so safe as she had claimed when she says to Antonio:

> The place that you must fly to is Ancona,
> Hire a house there. I'll send after you
> My treasure and my jewels: our weak safety
> Runs upon enginous wheels; short syllables
> Must stand for periods. I must now accuse you
> Of such a feigned crime as Tasso calls
> *Magnanima menzogna:* a noble lie
> 'Cause it must shield our honours.

(3. 2. 174–81)

After Bosola has tricked her into revealing her lie about Antonio's embezzlement and that Antonio is her husband, she agrees to let him devise a plan. Her desire to retain the honor she has forfeited guarantees the success of his argument. He counsels her:

> Feign a pilgrimage
> To Our Lady of Loretto, scarce seven leagues
> From fair Ancona; so may you depart
> Your country with *more honour,* and your flight
> *Will seem a princely progress* [my emphases], retaining
> Your usual train about you.

(3. 2. 307–12)

The Duchess is again in a position reminiscent of King Lear. He, too, wished to retain the honor and respect due to a ruler after he had resigned the responsibilities. Both Lear and the Duchess discover that without the responsibilities, the power, privilege, and prerogatives evaporate as well.

Between the scenes of her flight from Malfi and her banishment from Ancona, we are reminded again of the disastrous consequences for the common weal when rulers are "swayed by passion." As he sees Bosola hurry in to Ferdinand to reveal the secret of Antonio's identity, Pescara, whose function as vox populi figure recalls that of Lennox in *Macbeth* (Act 3, Scene 5), says:

> What should be the business?
> Some falling out amongst the cardinals.
> These factions amongst great men, they are like
> Foxes: when their heads are divided

> They carry fire in their tails, and all the country
> About them goes to wreck for't.
>
>   (3. 3. 35–40)

Given this judgment, it is paradoxically true that the Duchess's irresponsibility as duchess is what saves her country from being racked by war. But by deserting it and fleeing to Ancona, she makes herself, the head of state, completely vulnerable to her brothers, much as Mary Stuart made herself completely vulnerable to her cousin Elizabeth by fleeing to England after her defeat and imprisonment in Scotland.

Everything the Duchess has done to secure herself as Antonio's wife, however, has worked against her as duchess and wife. By placing her private desires above her public responsibility, she has forced herself into positions that have caused her to forfeit first order and decorum, then reputation, and, finally, freedom. By the end of Act 3, she has lost out as woman and as duchess; she is separated from husband and son and is a prisoner in the land she formerly ruled.

It seems to me that such ironic treatment of his central character implies that Webster has begun to weigh the Duchess, dramatically, against the values established in the play and to find her wanting. This is not to say that she is not on many levels an admirable character. So many critics have spent so much time analyzing and elaborating on the Duchess's virtues, as woman, that it would be redundant of me to add to her praises (especially in a study that attempts to establish that Webster's final judgment upon her is negative). Certainly he has done much to invite our sympathy for and, thus, our complicity with her. Yet the generic expectations and the action insist inexorably on her culpability as ruler, on her responsibility for her own fate, and, worse, for the disruption of her duchy. I do not insist that she is, in and of herself, evil but that, given the context, her choice and actions inevitably produce unintended and evil consequences.

Clearly, in Acts 2 and 3, we have begun to see Antonio's syllogistic prophecy fulfilled. To clarify the ways in which Acts 4 and 5 continue to imply the play's negative judgment on the Duchess and complete the syllogism, I would like to examine two other elements of Webster's rhetorical structure.

5

Unequal Nature

As I said in Chapter 1, the complexity of Webster's rhetoric has proved the major stumbling block to interpretation of *The Duchess of Malfi*. His elliptic use of generic conventions, juxtaposition of scenes, and imagistic echoes requires scrupulous attention in reading if we are to catch his rhetorical drift. For a modern audience, I think it would be virtually impossible to catch that drift in performance unless the production were informed by such a painstaking reading on the director's part. As I have said repeatedly, for Webster's audience familiarity with the genre, its assumptions, and the conventions informed by those assumptions would have made the significance of images and the implications of action and dialogue immediately apparent. But it is a tribute to Webster's art that the play is not so bound by time and place that it cannot yield up its rhetorical perspective to a close analysis of the articulation of its elements. We have seen the way Webster uses the image of poisoning the common fountain of government as a rhetorical metonymy and the use to which he puts analogy in the wooing scenes of Act 1. Two other examples of imagery and parodic analogy are especially worth analyzing because they, too, attest not only to the complexity but to the rhetorical coherence of the play.

A great deal of attention has been paid to natural imagery, particularly the imagery of animals, in *The Duchess of Malfi*. Once again, we are reminded of *King Lear,* and the reminder is pertinent because the animal imagery in Webster's play provides the same sort of comment on human nature and actions and establishes the same sort of thematic horizon as it does in Shakespeare's play. There are a number of analogies between these two works, as my constant comparisons imply, but one of the most striking is the relationship between themes and imagery.[1]

1. *King Lear* is repeatedly mentioned by critics in the course of discussing *The Duchess.* Ralph Berry's comment is typical: *"The Duchess of Malfi* should be studied as a play strongly influenced by *King Lear," The Art of John Webster,* p. 22. G. Wilson Knight, "The Duchess of Malfi," pp. 90–91, remarks in discussing the animal images in Webster's play that *"King Lear* is often suggested and Swift continually forecast." As my frequent use of Shakespeare's play for compara-

In both plays the ruler acts to satisfy a private desire and in so doing looses evil upon the ground of the play, and in both plays natural, animal imagery is used to comment upon the unnaturalness of that ruler's actions in human terms. With this imagery, Webster creates an ironic metaphorical context that companions the ethical-political context and in terms of which the Duchess's degeneration is measured at given points in the play.[2]

The Duchess's first lapse from responsibility is marked by her use of natural imagery: "Wish me good speed / For I am going into a wilderness, / Where I shall find nor path, nor friendly clew / To be my guide" (1. 1. 358–61). In other words, her metaphor suggests that she sees her passion, her desire for Antonio, as taking her into a wild, natural area outside the defined and regulated sphere of the community. The image takes on more pointed significance when she complains to Antonio that those born great "are forc'd to express our violent passions / In riddles, and in dreams, and leave the path / Of simple virtue, which was never made / To seem the thing it is not" (1. 1. 445–48). Thus, her initial departure from rank and degree is seen as a movement away from civilization—and virtue—into an unregulated, natural state. But here, as in *King Lear*, the question remains, is this state natural for man?[3]

A number of interpretations of the play see the Duchess's association with bird imagery as one of its means of approving her by identifying her with natural innocence. Standing as we do on the other side of the romantic era, we are more likely to see a character's association with nature as positive than negative. A Renaissance audience, of course, was likely to see quite the reverse. For them, this bird imagery might well mark the second step in the Duchess's movement away from the state natural to man and thus be one of the play's means of disapproving her. Implicitly, her initial desire is to be less than a duchess. As a result of the "violent passions" that prompted her

tive or illustrative material indicates, I believe *The Duchess* is remarkably influenced structurally, rhetorically, and thematically by *Lear*.

2. See Gunnar Boklund, *The Duchess of Malfi: Sources, Themes, Characters*, p. 118, and Robert Ornstein, *A Kingdom for a Stage: The Achievement of Shakespeare's History Plays*, p. 140.

3. Considering that civilization is identified with virtue and natural wilderness with disorder, it is not difficult to see how and why the (late) eighteenth and the nineteenth century could have misread both plays.

wish, and the marriage resulting from her desire, she does indeed cease to *be* a duchess, practically, when the Pope confiscates her duchy.

In her grief at being separated from Antonio, she seems to wish to be less than human: "The birds that live i' th' field / On the wild benefit of nature, live / Happier than we; for they may choose their mates, / And carol their sweet pleasures to the spring" (3. 5. 18–21). This suggests that she would resign her humanity in order to escape its responsibilities and restrictions. To the ears of Webster's audience, as Lagarde puts it, "to invoke the example of the birds of the field, as the heroine does, is to sin against the creation; man, being rational, is distinguished from the beasts in that he perceives the order willed by God."[4] However, it is not necessary to depend on such historical evidence, for within the same scene Webster provides two comments on this desire through other characters' use of animal imagery.

As Antonio takes leave of his wife, he counsels her to "be a good mother to your little ones, / And save them from the tiger" (3. 5. 85–86). This metaphor puts her understanding of the "wild benefit of nature" in a clear light by pointing to the savage aspect of the animal world. Mother birds are hardly a match for tigers and would, if a tiger could be bothered, be natural meat for them. There is a lively continuity here with the Duchess's earlier wilderness metaphor: By departing from the norms of a civilized community, she has moved into a wilderness in which there is no law but survival, no restrictions but those of instinct and appetite, and the weak are "naturally" devoured by the strong.

Webster has, of course, already shown and reminded us through the use of animal imagery (for example, Ferdinand as spider using the law as foul, black cobweb) that the Duchess's brothers are powerful, willful men, unrestrained by morality, ethics, religion, or law—the "natural" and institutional protectors of the weak in human community. By going out into her "wilderness," she has made herself prey to these tigers. That, however, is not enough to condemn her; obviously, as the response of many interpreters indicates, it is likely to make us sympathize with and fear for her, to see her as weak and vulnerable innocence. But, as I said, there is yet another use of animal

4. Fernand Lagarde, *John Webster*, 2:845, my translation.

imagery in this scene that makes Webster's perspective on her actions even clearer.

Bosola first enters the scene immediately after the Duchess's speech about the birds. He leaves as soon as he has delivered Ferdinand's letter, which lets her know that her brothers have learned Antonio's identity and that he is in danger from them. After Antonio's exit, Bosola returns to take the Duchess into custody. When he gives his order, "You must see your husband no more," she asks what "devil" he is that "counterfeits Heaven's thunder" (3. 5. 99–100). She refers, of course, to the sacramental nature of Christian marriage, to the heavenly nature of the bond that no man may put asunder. This retreat to the terms of the Christian institution of marriage jars strangely with her envy of the birds who mate without difficulties and restrictions, but as we have seen before, consistency is not the Duchess's strong suit. She means to insist on the human and religious dignity of her union with Antonio, but Bosola's rebuttal insists on the animalistically sensuous aspect of this particular marriage: "Is that terrible? I would have you tell me / Whether is that note worse that frights the silly birds / Out of the corn, or that which doth allure them / To the nets? you have hearken'd to the last too much" (3. 5. 101–4).

Granted, Bosola's analogy might say more about his characteristic reducing of the human to the animal level than about Webster's attitudes, but I think not. Bosola first enters the scene after the Duchess's speech about the birds, so he cannot be supposed to be consciously or associatively picking up her image and using it, sardonically, to put her down. Thus, it seems to me that the juxtaposition of the two speeches is a counter-balancing of the Duchess's perspective by Webster rather than, merely, a counterthrust by Bosola, presenting only his perspective. Because Bosola cannot know how appropriate and how telling his image is, we must, I think, assume that Webster is speaking through him here. What the speech says within the ironic metaphorical context is that her desire to mate as freely as the birds, her putting aside of human restrictions and forms in order to do so, is what entrapped her.

Invariably, the Duchess uses the bird imagery in self-defense or vindication and invariably it rebounds against her. Bosola's speech here recalls her first usage that initially pointed ironically to her failure to understand the implications and consequences of her action. In Act 3, Scene 2, when Ferdinand confronts her in her closet, she evidences again that misplaced self-confidence that led her to believe she could disregard "all discord" outside the circumference of her marriage: "Alas, your shears do come untimely now / To clip the bird's wings that's already flown!" (3. 2. 84–85). The bird may have flown, that is, she may have entered into a secret marriage without Ferdinand's approval, but he will show her that in consequence of the quality of that marriage, his "shears" still have the power to clip her wings and effectually "divorce" her from her husband.

Again, the imagery seems to insist on her culpability, her responsibility for her own fate, and her wrongheadedness. That she has moved one step farther away from her proper role and function is underlined when she rejects Bosola's claim that "your brothers mean you safety, and pity," saying: "Pity! / With such a pity men preserve alive / Pheasants and quails, when they are not fat enough / To be eaten" (3. 5. 110–13). This, of course, undercuts her earlier envy of the birds and recalls the effect of Antonio's tiger metaphor. She reinforces this in Act 4 when she refuses Cariola's attempts to comfort her: "Thou art a fool; / The robin-redbreast, and the nightingale, / Never live long in cages" (4. 2. 12–14). Ironically, she unconsciously admits that the natural state she coveted has drawbacks other than the presence of natural enemies. Songbirds, as well as pheasants and quail, must also fear man, the latter because man is as carnivorous as their natural enemies, the former because he may arbitrarily imprison them.

Identifying herself with innocent natural creatures is becoming characteristic to her. But the ironic metaphorical context makes it clear by charting her degeneration that she is not innocent and may not be "natural." She stepped away from the responsibility of rule in a desire to be simply human. She coveted the freedom of the animal state only to find herself as arbitrarily imprisoned as an animal might be. She has moved from the nobly human to the merely human, then to the non-human. In her final torments, her response will be, at least briefly, antihuman, revealing again her temperamental "kinship" with Ferdinand.

Ferdinand's characterization is more complex, I think, than has been noticed by some critics.[5] There can be no question that

5. See Boklund, *The Duchess of Malfi*, pp. 136–40 particularly.

he is a villain, that Webster paints him pretty black, but what is interesting to me is that evil as he may be, he shares more characteristics with the play's heroine than those of appearance. We have seen that Ferdinand wishes to act as motive force on the will of his courtiers (1. 1. 122–25), in other words, to control the world around him as though he were its center. Egocentricity is hardly a lovable trait, and Ferdinand's is virtually boundless. Webster provides him with natural images that act in the same ironic fashion as the Duchess's animal images to point out the radical quality of his egocentricity.

In Act 3, Scene 1, when discussing his plans to confront the Duchess in her chamber, Ferdinand refuses to tell Bosola exactly what he intends: "Do not ask then: / He that can compass me, and know my drifts, / May say he hath put a girdle 'bout the world / And sounded all her quicksands" (83–86). He could hardly have chosen a more self-revealing image nor have exposed the enormity of his ego more clearly than by seeing himself as having the depth and complexity of the natural world. Bosola bluntly and quietly corrects his vision by telling him what he thinks: "That you / Are your own chronicle too much; and grossly / Flatter yourself" (87–89).

Yet, although Bosola insists that Ferdinand not see himself as the whole world, given the generic assumptions and expectations, the duke's position makes his egocentricity more threatening than it would be in a private person. After all, he is capable of controlling and disrupting the world around him to a considerable degree. And his willingness to "batter down a goodly province" to revenge himself for a family grievance is the exact reverse of the proper relationship between will and the use of power in a ruler. This is made quite clear in his exchange, quoted earlier, with the Cardinal when he learns of the birth of the Duchess's child. When the Cardinal chides his rage by asking him why he makes himself such a tempest, Ferdinand replies, "Would I could be one." He wishes to be a tempest in order that he might "toss her palace 'bout her ears, / Root up her goodly forests, blast her meads, / And lay her general territory . . . waste" (2. 5. 16–20).[6]

6. Considering the pitch of erotic violence that Ferdinand works himself up to in this scene, it is interesting to conjecture if this speech is intended as a serious parody of the geography and topography of female sexual features, which Eric Partridge sees as one of Shakespeare's contributions to erotic literature (*Shakespeare's Bawdy,* pp. 6–7). If so, like Ferdinand's use of the Vulcan myth

Like the Duchess, Ferdinand is expressing himself with and through natural imagery, and, as they did to her, the images rebound against him ironically. Ferdinand would like to be turned into a natural force, a tempest, in order to destroy mead and forest. Thus, he would pervert nature by investing its power with malice. He would blast a "general territory" in order to vent his personal spleen. This desire to bring the world to chaos because it has not conformed to one's own expectations or beliefs is not merely egocentric, it is anarchic and antihuman.

In commonweal tragedy, speeches such as Ferdinand's invariably mark the degree to which the speaker has been corrupted by the force for disorder. Lear's speech on the heath is a typical example:[7]

> Blow, winds, and crack your cheeks! Rage! Blow!
> You cataracts and hurricanes, spout
> Till you have drench'd our steeples, drown'd the cocks!
> You sulph'rous and thought-executing fires,
> Vaunt-couriers of oak-cleaving thunderbolts,
> Singe my white head! And thou, all-shaking thunder,
> Strike flat the thick rotundity o' th' world!
> Crack nature's moulds, all germens spill at once
> That makes ingrateful man!
>
> (3. 2. 1–9)

Interestingly, and damningly, the Duchess's speeches in Act 4 are more radical than Ferdinand's and closer to the spirit of Lear. After she has been shown the wax figures that she believes to be the dead bodies of Antonio and her children, the Duchess longs to die. When a servant enters and wishes her long life, she takes his wish as a malediction. Then, in a paroxysm of despair

---

(1. 1. 313–16) it implies, once again, a basic erotic-incestuous preoccupation with his sister. In the Vulcan image, Ferdinand is warning the Duchess not to practice deceit, yet he himself has just spread a "fine small thread" of hypocrisy by putting Bosola in his sister's household to spy on her. Thus, unconsciously, he places himself in the position of Vulcan vis à vis the Duchess's Venus and Antonio's Mars.

7. For further examples see *Macbeth,* Act 4, Sc. 1, ll. 50–61, and *Antony and Cleopatra,* Act 1, Sc. 1, ll. 33–35; Act 2, Sc. 5, ll. 76–79; Act 4, Sc. 15, ll. 9–11. The first speech is Antony's, the second Cleopatra's; the earliness of these speeches in the play is indicative, I think, of the degree to which Shakespeare sees these rulers as already corrupted by the evil of placing their personal desires above the common weal—in this case the common weal of the entire world.

she decides that rather than pray she will "go curse." In the exchange with Bosola which follows, the Duchess reveals the depth of her anarchic egocentricity and a vengefulness that goes beyond justice, and certainly far beyond charity. Here, she shows the same sort of corruption by evil that brings Hamlet to want Claudius damned as well as dead:

> *Duch.*   I could curse the stars.
> *Bos.*   Oh fearful!
> *Duch.* And those three smiling seasons of the year
> Into a Russian winter, nay the world
> To its first chaos.
> *Bos.* Look you, the stars shine still:—
> *Duch.*   O, but you must
> Remember, my curse hath a great way to go.—
> Plagues, that make lanes through largest families,
> Consume them!—
> *Bos.*   Fie lady!
> *Duch.*   Let them, like tyrants,
> Never be remember'd, but for the ill they have done;
> Let all the zealous prayers of mortified
> Churchmen forget them!—
> *Bos.*   O, uncharitable!
> *Duch.* Let heaven, a little while, cease crowning martyrs,
> To punish them!

$$\text{(4. 1. 96–108)}$$

The lines require little explication. In her personal grief, the Duchess would blight the stars and condemn mankind to perpetual winter.[8] Yet, even that will not satisfy her. She would unmake the creation, reduce the world to un-being. Like her brother, she would invest a natural force, plague, with malice and, finally, she would seal up the springs of charity, grace, and mercy.

Certainly, she has had provocation: She has personally suffered great and seemingly gratuitous cruelty at the hands of her brother, and she believes her husband and children to have been murdered by, or at least at the behest of, that same brother. But the hint of ranting in her curse and the nihilism of her desire to reduce all of nature and mankind to the "first chaos" go beyond excess of grief. In a manner not only metaphorical, they recall, affectively, Cariola's first judgment of her mistress's actions—"fearful madness." I would like to return

8. See K. H. Ansari, *John Webster: Image Patterns and Canon*, p. 124.

later to the significance of Webster's bringing together the theme of madness and the imagery of nature, but it seems to me that in using the natural images here, Webster extends the ironic metaphorical context and allows the Duchess to reveal in her cosmic "anti-design," on an exaggerated scale, the egocentricity that drove her to place her private desire above her responsibility to the little world in which her will could effect chaos. By the end of Act 4, Scene 1, we can see how Webster has used this ironic metaphorical context to comment upon the Duchess's gradual degeneration. She has arrived at a position that is the diametrical opposite of that which she held, in name at least, at the beginning of the action. She has moved from the nobly human to, briefly, the antihuman. In terms of the ethical-political values of the play, she has become an anti-ruler whose will is turned to the destruction of order rather than to its creation, or, at least, its preservation.

In light of this, I think it hardly possible to say that "when the Duchess lies dead with her children, violence has been done not only to innocence but also to nature."[9] On the contrary, it seems to me that it is she who did violence to human nature, and the natural imagery tends to underline this. If common human beings may not live like the birds, much less may those responsible for ruling other human beings. After all, wolves are as natural as birds, and this is the point of Ferdinand's lycanthropy. In the metaphorical context, Ferdinand becomes a living metaphor. His will to power, his cruelty, his desire to destroy and consume find their natural analogue in the behavior of the wolf. The Duchess's gentleness, sweetness, and desire for "natural" sexuality find theirs in the behavior of the birds. But in the natural world, the bird is a weak creature and the wolf a voracious one. The bird is incapable even of self-protection and the wolf is likely to consume those around him. Thus, Webster uses these natural images to reveal both unnatural aspects of human behavior and the characteristics that make the Duchess and Ferdinand most unfit for rule. Rather than elevating her, the animal imagery works to diminish the Duchess.

It is tellingly indicative of the negative connotations of the bird imagery that before the Duchess's initial comparison of herself to the bird that had flown, only Bosola and the Cardinal mention birds or employ bird images. Bosola compares the

9. Boklund, *The Duchess of Malfi,* p. 118.

sycophants surrounding the brothers to "crows" and "daws," and later, during the Duchess's confinement, he wonders whether the shriek he hears is a woman's or an owl's (2. 3. 1–9). The way in which this latter occasion prepares for the next use of the bird image is uncanny—as though Webster were allowing the terms of his metaphor to converge almost magnetically across the play's linguistic surface. Here, Bosola has difficulty distinguishing the woman's cry from the bird's. In the next scene the Cardinal collapses the distinction and uses the voracity of the bird of prey to characterize Julia's sexuality: "I have taken you off your melancholy perch, / Bore you upon my fist, and show'd you game, / And let you fly at it" (2. 4. 28–30). As the first metaphor of woman as bird this unquestionably colors our response to the Duchess's repeated use of those metaphors just discussed.

Again there is an uncanny suitability in this that attests to the complexity and the coherence of Webster's rhetoric. Just as the Cardinal's use of the bird image to characterize Julia's sexuality undercuts the Duchess's later images, so Julia herself provides an analogical undercutting of the Duchess's behavior in her own actions.[10]

The technique of analogical definition is, of course, a structural convention of Renaissance drama. The variety, flexibility, and complexity of this technique are apparent, but one of the simplest and best known instances will serve to clarify my sense of its workings. In *Dr. Faustus,* Marlowe has created the characters of Wagner and Robin, whose sole function in the play is to define Faustus's aspirations and actions through parody. Obviously, the parody is Marlowe's, not Wagner's or Robin's. The servants and clowns intend only to emulate Faustus's actions, but their attitudes toward his magic, the ends to which they would put it, and the results of their attempts to dabble in it reveal parodically the quality of Faustus's interests, desires, and actions. Webster uses Julia for the same purpose in *The Duchess of Malfi.* The difference is that in Webster's play the parodic action is not comic; both means and ends of the parody are quite serious.

10. Of course, a number of critics have seen Julia as comment on the Duchess. Berry, *The Art of John Webster,* pp. 38–41, also uses the example from *Dr. Faustus* to exemplify the technique. Thus far no one has attempted to explicate the effect as fully as I have here. See Lagarde, *John Webster,* 2:851, 915; John Russell Brown, ed., *The Duchess of Malfi,* p. xli; Boklund, *The Duchess of Malfi,* p. 78; Clive Hart, ed., *The Duchess of Malfi,* p. 7.

If we fail to recognize that this is Julia's function, I think we would have to concur with Lewis Theobald's implicit judgment that Julia is an expendable element in the play. In 1723 Theobald published a reworking of the play entitled *The Fatal Secret.* There is no Julia in this revision. That omission and other of Theobald's changes indicate a number of things. The most obvious, of course, is an eighteenth-century impatience with the unclassical, double-plot structure of Renaissance drama. Webster's mirror plot, of which Julia is the "heroine," must have seemed to Theobald a typical (and typically nasty) corruption of form in the plays of virtually all the dramatists of the period —even, alas, Shakespeare's.

It is understandable that the eighteenth-century preference for classical form might result in an inability to appreciate, or even understand, the paratactic articulation (to borrow Auerbach's term) of English Renaissance drama. But it is more difficult to understand what changes in morals, manners, or ethics had come about that would allow Theobald to spare the Duchess and Antonio at the end of the play in the name of poetic justice. This alteration, like the omission of Julia, implies that the reviser and his age had already lost the generic expectations, if not the doctrinal assumptions, which would clarify and ratify the play's internal standards. Julia could only have been regarded as superfluous if her function were not clearly apprehended and/or the play's judgment on the Duchess were not understood.

The number and timing of Julia's appearances in the play point to her function as parodic foil. She and the Duchess make their first appearance on stage together in Act 1.[11] She merely walks on with the Cardinal, Cariola, and the Duchess, remains on stage for the duration of some hundred lines, and walks off with the Duchess, Cariola, and miscellaneous courtiers. Among them is Castruchio, her husband, but not even this relationship is revealed, nor is the fact of her liaison with the Cardinal. We might legitimately wonder what the logic of her appearance is.

---

11. In Brown's edition, Julia enters before the Duchess (line 82). Other editors, for example Elizabeth Brennan *(The Duchess of Malfi)*, have them enter together. I think the effect I speak of is strengthened if they do enter together; also, having Julia make her first appearance with the Cardinal and not her husband prepares the audience for Act 2, Sc. 4, which would keep the director from having to go to the lengths of that recent BBC production in order to imply the nature of the relationship. In that production the Cardinal and Julia are post-coitus, still in bed when the scene opens, which was rather a nice touch, however.

Dramatically, Webster does no more with her at this point. Yet, unless we are to imagine that he simply wants to swell the crowd on stage, it would seem a legitimate conclusion that his primary purpose has to do with the visual impact of her appearing with the Duchess. They never appear on stage together again, but by means of this initial appearance, Webster has, visually at least, suggested an association between them.

Julia remains no more than a "shadow" of the Duchess in the audience's memory until Act 2, Scene 4; but when she returns the visual association is reinforced verbally, and Webster's analogical reduction of the Duchess through Julia begins. Nothing else impels Julia into the play at this point. Nothing in the scene preceding causes her appearance nor her exchanges with the Cardinal and Delio, nor does her presence cause or affect the action that follows. The announcement of the arrival of Delio and Castruchio at the Cardinal's palace and a servant's report that the duke is much moved by the letter Castruchio brings from Bosola are the only matters bearing on the main plot. Yet, these things are reported incidentally and would hardly require a scene at any rate. The scene focuses on Julia, and the question is why, at a very crucial point of the action, Webster should reintroduce Julia and put her into the spotlight.

Perhaps the answer may be suggested by reviewing the structural and thematic development of the play to this point. The Duchess's secret marriage has begun to have chaotic effects on her court. Her child has been born prematurely, and, unable to remove herself from the palace, she and Antonio concoct a story of theft, as justification for locking everyone in his room overnight. Unfortunately, Antonio has dropped the horoscope he cast for the newborn child and given Bosola irrefutable proof of the Duchess's cohabitation, if not of her secret marriage. In the thematic development, the leveling of degree desired by the Duchess in order to favor her husband has, ironically, come about not in the matter of ceremony but in the reputation and very quality of the Duchess and Antonio. The latter's own comment is that *"The great are like the base—nay, they are the same —/ When they seek shameful ways, to avoid shame"* (2. 3. 51–52). With that aside, Antonio leaves the stage, and the horoscope, to Bosola. Bosola's discovery causes him to identify Antonio as "the Duchess' Bawd" and to remark of her, *"Though lust do mask in ne'er so strange disguise, / She's oft found witty, but is never wise"* (2. 3. 76–77).

Antonio's lines sum up his sense of the effect that their actions have had upon himself and the Duchess. They are lying
to keep the world from discovering her condition. To Antonio,
such mendacity is shameful and has brought them down to the
level of the "base." To Bosola, the leveling agency is "lust." The
next scene provides a comment upon both these judgments
through Julia's exchange with the Cardinal. She, too, is using
lies in order to keep her good name, and in the service of lust:

> Card.   Prithee tell me
>   What trick didst thou invent to come to Rome
>   Without thy husband.
> Jul.   Why, my lord, I told him
>   I came to visit an old anchorite
>   Here, for devotion.
> Card.   Thou are a *witty false* [my emphasis]
>   one:—
>   I mean to him.
>
>   (2. 4. 1–6)

The juxtaposition of Bosola's closing comment on the Duchess's lust-born wit and the Cardinal's appreciation of Julia's wit
can hardly be accidental.[12] It establishes an analogy between
the Duchess's motivation and actions and Julia's or, to put it in
Antonio's terms, between the "great" and the "base." Without
Antonio's speech, we might simply see Bosola's lines as characteristic of him, but the juxtaposition of speeches enforces the
analogy.

Once again, Webster is setting up grids against which to
measure the Duchess's actions and to reinforce generic expectations. Despite her attempts to justify her passion for Antonio
through a dubious legality, there is no question that passion—
unkindly called "lust" by Bosola—motivated her. In Julia's exchange with the Cardinal, Webster provides a "base" analogue
of the Duchess's self-justifications (and a prefiguration of her
later use of religion as "her riding-hood," which Lagarde,
among others, has seen as damning).[13]

12. See Lagarde, *John Webster,* 2:851. He notes the juxtaposition of the "witty-
wise" diction and its effect, then goes on: "Mais la juxtaposition est cruelle à
plus d'un égard; la sensualité vulgaire de Julia n'est pas un simple repoussoir
à l'honnê-teté de la passion de l'héroïne; elle en est aussi une charge fèroce,
annonçant le sort qui guette toute femme quand la raison a cédé le pas à
l'instinct."
13. Ibid., p. 853.

Stung by the Cardinal's remark, Julia counters by saying, "You have prevail'd with me / Beyond my strongest thoughts: I would not now / Find you inconstant" (2. 4. 6–8). In other words, she is a constant woman whose lapse is understandable given its object, the Cardinal, whose rhetoric overcame her reason. He reduces her argument brutally by accusing her of (a classical, Freudian) projection: "Do not put thyself / To such a voluntary torture, which proceeds / Out of your own guilt" (2. 4. 8–10). When she attempts to stand on her record of fidelity to him, he goes on to generalize about the general inconstancy of the sex and to point out that her tears are no justification; in other words, she may not rely upon feminine frailty to justify her trespass. Finally, when she threatens to return to virtue— or at least to her husband—the Cardinal strips her poor ego of its last vestige of dignity:

> You may thank me, lady,
> I have taken you off your melancholy perch,
> Bore you upon my fist, and show'd you game,
> And let you fly at it:—I pray thee kiss me—
> When thou wast with thy husband, thou was watch'd
> Like a tame elephant:—still you are to thank me—
> Thou hadst only kisses from him, and high feeding,
> But what delight was that? 'twas just like one
> That hath a little fing'ring on the lute,
> Yet cannot tune it:—still you are to thank me.

>   (2. 4. 27–36)

In this wonderfully cruel, graphic speech, Webster further underlines the analogy between Julia and the Duchess. The Duchess saw herself variously as songbird, pheasant, and quail. Repeatedly and ironically, the images rebounded against her to reveal wherein she failed in logic and in responsibility and, thus, exactly how important sexuality was to her. She unconsciously revealed her sexuality by choosing the bird images, but the Cardinal consciously uses the metaphor of a bird of prey to force Julia to accept that her liaison with him is motivated by animalistic, instinctive, and voracious lust. However, this is the Cardinal's judgment and his quality is already apparent. Since Julia continues to insist that her weakness was caused by love for him and his professed need for her, there is still some ambiguity, at least for modern audiences, concerning Julia's exact quality. The exchange with Delio that follows removes some of

this ambiguity and reinforces what would have been understood by a Renaissance audience from the very fact of her
liaison.

At Delio's entrance, Julia's aside informs us that he was one
of her suitors before her marriage to Castruchio. Finding her
now in the Cardinal's palace, Delio assumes that she need no
longer be regarded as an honest woman and offers her money:

> Jul.   I must hear the condition, ere I be bound to take it.
> Delio. Look on't, 'tis gold—hath it not a fine colour?
> Jul.   I have a bird more beautiful.
> Delio. Try the sound on't.
> Jul.   A lute-string far exceeds it.
>
> (2. 4. 60–63)

Julia's banter might be innocent if we, like Delio, had not heard
the Cardinal's speech in which Julia was compared to bird and
lute (and were not aware of the connotation of birds and of
playing on instruments in Renaissance bawdy). When she says
"I have a bird more beautiful" and "A lute-string far exceeds
it," she seems to be vaunting her value as a bed partner—given
the terms of the Cardinal's metaphors. Whether she intends it
or not, the implication is that he simply has not offered enough
to purchase such value (and this is borne out by her next appearance in the play). Once again, Webster is creating an ironic
metaphorical context by means of which he can imply value
judgments on his characters.

The negative judgment on Julia is reinforced when Delio tells
her bluntly what his suit is:

> Delio.   I would wish you
>   (At such time as you are non-resident
>   With your husband) my mistress.
> Jul.   Sir, I'll go ask my husband if I shall,
>   And straight return your answer. [Exit.]
> Delio.   Very fine!
>   Is this her wit or honesty that speaks thus [my emphasis]?
>
> (2. 4. 72–77)

Given the terms of the choice here, the audience cannot remain
uncertain of the answer. We know, as Delio does not, that she
is the Cardinal's mistress, and, therefore, it is not her "honesty"
that speaks. We must accept the first alternative: She is wittily
using language to conceal her real quality in the world of the

play, but Webster is using it to insist on that quality for the audience.

The question of her wit returns us to Bosola's comment on the Duchess and recalls the analogy between the two women. Julia has managed to use her wit to deceive her husband and Delio about her honesty. Whether she will remain both witty and wise, in pursuing her lust, is still an open question, but the atmosphere created by this scene underscores the Duchess's lack of wisdom, or, at least, forethought. In such a world, Bosola's news of the birth of her child will invite only one kind of interpretation. That she could be unaware or careless of the quality of this world and its perceptions, as she was careless of the power and unscrupulousness of her brothers, is an indication of her lack of wisdom.

Through this scene in which he examines Julia, Webster reinforces his negative judgment of the Duchess by analogy and by the further delineation of the context of her actions. Antonio had said that the great are like the base when they seek shameful ways to avoid shame. Webster then provides us, in the picture of Julia-as-adultress, with a neat little example of the base to illustrate his point. The analogy between the Duchess's and Julia's passion and deception seems to bear out Antonio's *sententia* and to imply a "baseness" in the Duchess that cannot be ameliorated by an appeal to her love or her frailty. Both Julia and the Duchess have stepped outside the law to satisfy their passions—Julia in committing adultery; the Duchess in substituting a private pact for a legal and public bond. Julia's moral quality may seem infinitely inferior to the Duchess's—her desires more base, and her deception more sinful—but by isolating passion and deceit in Julia, stripped of all the sweetness of character, charming domesticity, and private legalism that would seem to justify the Duchess, Webster insists on the "baseness" of the latter's motivation and, thus, on her greater culpability as ruler.[14] How inexorably he insists on this will be seen in the uses to which he puts Julia in Act 5, after the Duchess's death in Act 4.

There is no denying the affective power of Act 4 of *The Duchess of Malfi*.[15] For a full act, we are involved with the Duchess; we

14. James L. Calderwood, "*The Duchess of Malfi:* Styles of Ceremony," p. 137.
15. I realize that some critics do deny it any value, but it seems to me that the very vehemence of their condemnation argues for its power to affect. Recently, virtually all of the "excesses" of Act 4 have been defended on one

watch her suffer horribly—apparently out of all proportion to any "sins" she may have committed. We see her pass through sadness, frenzy, and despair to the achievement of serene resignation and hope of salvation at her death. She has endured so much that even the cynical Bosola, who had earlier reminded her crudely that she was too much concerned with lust, sees her as innocence itself (and with precisely the sort of image she used to insist on the innocence and legitimacy of her desires): "O, she's gone again: there the cords of life broke. / O sacred innocence, that sweetly sleeps / On turtles' feathers" (4. 2. 354–56). Beyond this appearance of innocence, Webster has given her a kind of pathetic stature through her suffering and final Christian-Stoic acceptance of death.

It would be tempting at that point to absolve the Duchess of all guilt, of all responsibility for the past. Those who insist that she may be so absolved and that this is the moment when the play should logically end miss Webster's point—and the point of commonweal tragedy. However much Ferdinand's eyes may dazzle or Bosola's fill with tears at her beauty in death, the sight is hidden from the world at large. However much stature she may have acquired through her suffering and resignation, she has acquired it solely as an individual, not as a prince.

It might be asked then exactly how Act 4 fits into Webster's rhetorical structure or accords with the generic expectations raised by commonweal tragedy. I have no intention of mounting a full discussion or defense of Act 4 here. The word *defense* suggests itself irresistibly because most treatments that try to fit it neatly into critical schema have come to exactly that—apologetic and/or ingenious defense. Nevertheless, I do think that a case can be made for its rational purpose and function in the play—if not for the absolute integrity of its construction—and

---

ground or another. A good explication of the madmen and their place can be found in Cecil W. Davies's "The Structure of *The Duchess of Malfi:* An Approach," pp. 92–93. Probably the least arbitrary comment is Berry's: "Let us clarify the matter. The primary purpose of the waxworks and the dead hand is not to horrify us; it is to horrify the Duchess. The fourth act is about the prolonged mental torture of the Duchess; her reactions are what constitute the drama," see his work, *The Art of John Webster,* p. 20. In other words, the waxworks, dead hand, and madmen have the effect, if not the intention, of a play within a play, much like Hamlet's play. Given Berry's logic it makes as much sense to criticize the "mousetrap" as a bad play. Nevertheless, as I shall argue, the act does have something to contribute to the overall rhetorical structure.

I would like to discuss it briefly before returning to Webster's use of Julia as parodic analogy in Act 5.

There can be little question that in Act 4 Webster was straining after spectacular effects that have, at given points, only the most tenuous connection with his larger rhetorical and dramatic purposes. Unfortunately, for modern theater audiences, I think even the spectacle fails to achieve the fearsome thrills he aimed for by mixing humor and horror because contemporary attitudes often cause reversal of these responses. The dead hand dropped or flung to the stage lands with a disconcerting thud, and the figures of the Duchess's family recall the wax museum too ludicrously to validate her frenzied grief. Worse, it is difficult for a twentieth-century audience, conditioned to think of insanity as mental illness, to laugh at madmen, without some twinge of guilt. Worst of all, to move so quickly from the grisly humor of the madmen to the garroting of the Duchess requires a leap that our own experience with theater and film has not prepared us to make in tragedy. (Even in recent productions that do yoke the pathetic and satiric, the self-consciousness of presentation, and response, argues for the novelty of such yoking for us.) Therefore, much of the critical dismay with Act 4, which led Shaw, for example, to sneer at Webster as "Tussaud laureate," has apparently resulted from cultural and conventional changes over the years.

I do not mean to imply by this argument that the act is without inherent flaws. The basic problem revolves around the question of efficient cause. How are we to account for or accept the means of bringing the Duchess to her death? What is the dramatic justification for the stage business leading up to it? Since Ferdinand is the motive force and Bosola the immediate agent of her torment and death, the question for most critics has come down to reconciling their motivations and characterizations with the action. Why does Ferdinand want her tormented and killed precisely this way, and how can Bosola act as his agent when his own changing attitude toward the Duchess clearly conflicts with so acting? The explanations put forth are legion, and it would be beside my purpose to cite or sort them out here. Especially since I have not made up my mind whether Webster gives us sufficient evidence to reconcile the motives and actions of the two men. We may simply have to take their own explanations at face value: Ferdinand wants her punished for disobeying his wishes and violating the family honor;

Bosola still hopes for some sort of reward for services rendered. That, however, does not answer the original question about efficient cause.

The answer seems to me that just as Webster had allowed Ferdinand and the Cardinal to "speak for" the play in Act 1, here he lets Ferdinand and Bosola "act in behalf of" the play in ways for which he unfortunately does not provide sufficiently clear motivation to satisfy us. What the Duchess receives from Ferdinand and Bosola, acting to establish the play's rhetorical perspective, is *condign punishment*.[16] Such an interpretation can only be considered, however, if we pay close attention to the way in which theme, image, and action are woven together in Act 4.

We saw how the use of animal imagery by the Duchess and the others rebounded against her ironically. She intended to insist on her innocence and her misfortune in being unable to choose her mate and live as freely as the birds of the field. Instead, Webster constructed the metaphorical context so that these images implied her culpability in wishing to evade the responsibility of rule. They also implied the madness of any human's desiring a return to the wild state in which the strong may prey on the weak.

In Scene 2 of Act 4, the Duchess sees her incarceration in animal terms again (ll. 13–14), implying that she is as innocent of guilt and as arbitrarily imprisoned by human cruelty as a caged songbird. Yet, immediately before this she had delivered a curse so ranting and nihilistic that it recalled Cariola's first judgment of her mistress's actions. Cariola saw the Duchess's secret marriage as the manifestation of "a fearful madness." If radical inappropriateness of behavior in a given context and given circumstances can be characterized as madness, the consequences of this marriage bear out that judgment. Because she pursued her desire for a state like the birds'—regardless of its inappropriateness to her rank and responsibility and her kind—she made herself as vulnerable to superior force as they. In a sense, then, the natural imagery implies that she has received no more than austere justice in her imprisonment.

Her assertion that she is "not mad yet" (4. 2. 24) is brought into question not only by the imagery and the consequences of

16. Paul Jorgensen's discussion of spectacular art and condign punishment in *Macbeth,* and on the Jacobean stage generally, in *Our Naked Frailties* was very instructive to me in analyzing the nature of Act 4.

her actions but by its immediate juxtaposition with the mad-men. As she sits giving forced audience to the lunatic masque, the scene becomes both a caricature of and a comment on her previous behavior as ruler. Her refusal to place public responsi-bility above personal desires has resulted in her becoming a princess of misrule over a court of antics. When she had the power to rule, to purge her court of "flatt'ring sycophants, of dissolute / And infamous persons," to reduce her state "to a fix'd order," she turned instead to personal pleasures. Now she is powerless even to order from her presence creatures appar-ently driven mad by their dissolute and corrupt practices. Thus, she is, in a sense, as much a prisoner of her own madness as they are. Certainly, having just held reluctant court over such sub-jects in the place where she should rule undercuts the supposed sublimity of "I am Duchess of Malfi still."

What further undercuts it is the secret nature and sordid manner of her death. (Strangulation is after all not a mode of execution befitting a prince, even if the play is set in a Jacobean Englishman's idea of Italy.) Here again, Ferdinand and Bosola act as agents of condign punishment, implying the play's rhe-torical perspective on its heroine. The private nature of her marriage denied the responsibility of rule that public ceremony recognizes and subverted the respect of rulers that it enhances. Similarly, the birth of a ruler's children usually occasions public and ceremonial rejoicing, but the birth of the Duchess's and Antonio's children must be a backstairs matter that they fear-fully keep secret. Thus, by having her killed in the night, hid-den from all but her tormentors, Ferdinand simply follows the precedent she has set. His own desire may be for personal or familial vengeance, and the manner of her death suggested by fear, guilt, madness, or whatever, but in the larger rhetorical structure of the play, and in light of the generic assumptions of commonweal tragedy, it further implies her culpability as a ruler.

The similarity of circumstance (though not, of course, of method) to Mary Stuart's execution is striking—and instruc-tive. Elizabeth's counsellors quite purposefully kept the pro-ceedings private and remote. Not even Mary knew the exact time until it was virtually upon her. Almost all her attendants had been driven away, and there was no more of an audience than was needed to give the proceedings an air of legality. A most telling touch was that all of Mary's household were held incommunicado at Fotheringay until the burial should take place—and that was postponed from February until the end of July. One purpose of all these precautions was that there be no demonstration of public mourning that would dignify Mary's death as that of a queen. Another was that there be no publicity, no account of the courageous and Christian manner in which Mary met her death. The world was not to see Mary's death as Mary herself had come to anticipate it, as a Christian martyrdom. The English government wanted no such image to erase the image created, especially in Catholic Europe, by Mary's apparent complicity in Darnley's death, her "abduction" by Bothwell, and the scandalous marriage to her abductor. Thus, the effects of her behavior were not countered by her personal nobility in death.[17] The same is true of the Duchess.

She had been isolated from the world of the play since the end of Act 3, and her death cannot erase the effects enabled or caused by her willful action. The final act of *The Duchess of Malfi* may seem as inexplicably concerned with matters unrelated to its protagonist as does the final act of *King Lear*. Without the business of this final act, however, the action of each play would be radically altered and its rhetorical thrust blunted. It is Webster's point, as it is Shakespeare's, that the protagonist may experience his own redemptive suffering and his personal anagnorisis, but that does not halt the forces set in motion by his initial blindness and willful action in the world of the play.

If we had forgotten the nature of that world while watching the Duchess's imprisonment, torture, and death, alone at Malfi, we are forcefully reminded at the opening of Act 5. Webster's use of contrast here is jolting and marvellously effective. The first thing that confronts us is her husband, for love of whom she threw a world into chaos, bereft of land and living in fear of his life. She may have escaped this world, but he must still live in it and with the consequences of her actions. Delio, never given to optimism in the play, paints for Antonio and the audience a black picture of Antonio's situation. (We, of course, are aware that Antonio has even greater cause for sorrow than he knows.) He still hopes there may be a possibility for reconciliation with the Duchess's brothers, but Delio insists on the vanity of that hope. They still play the consummate hypocrites whose

17. See Antonia Fraser, *Mary Queen of Scots*, pp. 540, 543–44, 548, and Agnes Strickland, *The Life of Mary Queen of Scots*, vol. 2, pp. 415, 456, 462–65, for accounts of the arrangements before and after Mary's death.

"letters of safe conduct . . . appear / But nets to trap you" (5. 1. 3–5). Even the good people are forced to evil actions against Antonio because of the circumstances created by the Duchess. As Delio informs him:

> The Marquis of Pescara,
> Under whom you hold certain land in cheat,
> Much 'gainst his noble nature, hath been mov'd
> To seize those lands, and some of his dependants
> Are at this instant making it their suit
> To be invested in your revenues.
> I cannot think they mean well to your life
> That do deprive you of your means of life,
> Your living.
>
> (5. 1. 5–13)

This seizure of Antonio's lands at the instigation of the Duchess's brothers might have had topical significance for Jacobeans. In 1609, six years after Raleigh's imprisonment in the tower, James, quite arbitrarily, seized his estate at Sherbourne. "Feeling ran high against his act. Lady Raleigh went on her knees before the King and begged to be spared this much out of her husband's ruin, but James, muttering 'I maun have the land, I maun have it for Carr' refused her."[18] Raleigh could well have heeded Delio's warning that he could not "think they mean well to your life / That do deprive you of your means of life, / Your living"; he was, of course, eventually executed by James on a charge of high treason.

Of more relevance to the play, however, are the persons who are ultimately enriched by these acts of tyranny. Raleigh's land was seized in order to gratify James's apparently boundless appetite for bestowing gifts and titles on his favorite, Robert Carr. Antonio's is bestowed similarly. To validate his assessment of the situation for Antonio, Delio petitions the Marquis for a part of the land but is refused. Immediately, Julia enters and is now identified as the Cardinal's mistress—apparently she has not been witty or wise enough to continue to fool the world. She comes with a letter from the Cardinal to second her request for the same land that Delio has just been refused. Pescara grants her suit, explaining to Delio that he could not bestow land upon a friend "not forfeited / By course of law, but ravish'd from [Antonio's] throat / By the cardinal's entreaty."

18. G. P. V. Akrigg, *Jacobean Pageant or the Court of King James I,* p. 180.

This, he says, is "gratification / Only due to a strumpet." Pescara is glad that "this land, ta'en from the owner by such wrong, / Returns again unto so foul an use / As salary for his lust" (5. 1. 41–52).

There is an interesting ambiguity of reference in that last "his." Ostensibly, Pescara means it to refer to the Cardinal; yet, the nearest possible antecedent is "the owner," that is, Antonio. I wonder if Webster had an ironic purpose in allowing this obscurity to stand. Antonio had told the Duchess, "I have long serv'd virtue, / And ne'er ta'en wages of her," and she had replied, "Now she pays it!" (1. 1. 439–40). In other words, she invited Antonio to see her hand as his overdue reward for being a virtuous man. On a strictly Christian level, this was, of course, presumptuous of her, but his acquiescence indicated his willingness to have that virtue so rewarded. Now, because he gratified her desires, his land has become salary for the gratification of the Cardinal's desires. Because the marriage that grew out of their passion caused the Duchess to be called "strumpet," Antonio's land becomes "wages" for the Cardinal's "strumpet." Thus, in a deeply ironic sense, the "foul" use to which Antonio's land "returns" is salary for his own "lust"—whether sexual passion or, as Delio says, "ambition" (2. 4. 81).

By making the Duchess's desire for Antonio result finally in his impoverishment and the enrichment of a "strumpet," Webster provides as certain a reductive comment upon her actions as the analogy created in Act 2, Scene 4. However, the ultimate reduction takes place in Act 5, Scene 2, in Julia's wooing of Bosola. I discussed earlier the way in which shape and diction of the scenes in which the Duchess wooed Antonio and Ferdinand "wooed" Bosola suggested an analogy between their actions and, thereby, a negative judgment on the Duchess. This analogy worked subtly through the structural tension between plot, character, and theme. The analogy between Julia's wooing of Bosola and the Duchess's wooing of Antonio is more obvious because not only shape and diction of the scenes are similar but motivations, means, and ends as well. In other words, this analogy works parodically rather than metaphorically, and, thus, its rhetoric is more obvious and its judgment more apparent.[19]

Both women admit to unwomanly behavior in wooing men. The Duchess insisted on her reluctance to violate decorum,

19. See Lagarde, *John Webster,* p. 915.

claiming that only the restrictions placed on her by rank would force her to such unconventional behavior. Yet surely the disparity between her rank and Antonio's could not explain away the urgency and haste with which she brought the secret marriage to its consummation.[20] In that spoke something other than the exigencies of greatness. The structure and diction of Julia's scene suggest analogically, and pitilessly, what the something other was. Julia's excuse for accosting Bosola, despite his obvious inferiority to her in beauty, is a piece of pretty fraudulence. She accuses him of bribing one of her women to put "Love-powder" in her drink, reasoning "Why should I fall in love with such a face else?" (l. 158). To make the effects of this powder clear to Bosola and thus insist on the precise nature of her urgency, she tells him: "I have already suffr'd for thee so much pain, / The only remedy to do me good / Is to kill my longing" (ll. 159–61). Thus, explicitly and from the outset, Webster insists that Julia is controlled by a kind of sexual "madness," a madness that corresponds to that discerned by Cariola in the Duchess's behavior.

Her immodesty and directness make Julia's behavior a wanton parody of the Duchess's behavior. But the continued correspondence between the scenes implies that a similar imperative reinforces the willfulness of these women. Just as Antonio had insisted on his "unworthiness" in relation to the Duchess's rank and beauty, Bosola implies his inferiority to Julia, seeing her attraction to him as "wondrous strange." He objects that he is a "blunt soldier" who "wants compliment"; in other words, he lacks the qualities that would make him her equal in "Courtship." Just as the Duchess countered by claiming that Antonio's personal worth overcame their disparity in rank, Julia answers Bosola by claiming that these apparent disabilities are actually virtues that compensate for his lack of polish (ll. 173–77). After Antonio had given in to her wooing, the Duchess gently scolded him for not having "begg'd" the kiss she had bestowed. Julia

20. Two antithetical responses to the same bit of action: Leonora Leet Brodwin takes the Duchess's offer to place a sword between herself and Antonio absolutely straight: "If ever there was a love that could be dissociated from lust, it is that of the Duchess," Leonora Leet Brodwin, *Elizabethan Love Tragedy, 1587–1625*, p. 287. In contrast, Eloise K. Goreau says, "It is perfectly clear that Antonio and the Duchess are marrying as a remedy against burning. The Duchess's mind is very much on the consummation of the marriage in the first act; and in the third, Antonio's is very much on carnal temptation," Eloise K. Goreau, *Integrity of Life: Allegorical Imagery in the Plays of John Webster,* p. 147.

more directly expresses her dissatisfaction with Bosola's back-
wardness: "You will mar me with commendation, / Put yourself to the charge of courting me / Whereas now I woo you"
(5. 2. 181–83).

As Antonio had done, Bosola questions the danger in the
relationship, and Julia dismisses that danger (significantly
represented by one or both of the Duchess's brothers in each
case) as lightly as the Duchess had done. In both scenes, the
women make clear that their reluctant suitors have something
to gain besides their persons and, in both cases, insist on haste
in confirming their affections. Julia asserts her haste bluntly:
"We that are *great women of pleasure* [my emphasis], use to cut off
/ These uncertain wishes, and unquiet longings, / And in an
instant join the sweet delight / And the pretty excuse together;
had you been i'th' street, / Under my chamber window, even
there / I should have courted you" (ll. 193–98).

Surely, it is no accident that her diction should recall and
simultaneously parody the Duchess's pathetic cry: "The misery
of us that are born great. / We are forced to woo because none
dare woo us." Nor can it be accidental that Bosola should show
surprise at Julia's urgency, as Antonio had done at the Duchess's, and that she should send him into her chamber, as the
Duchess had asked Antonio to lead the way to hers. Julia makes
no pretense about her desires and her haste to have them sa-
tisfied. She lusts for Bosola; the impetuosity and the precipi-
tousness of her actions are dictated by her lust, and those actions bring about her destruction as surely as the Duchess's
actions bring about hers. In Julia's case the compression of the
action makes the cause-and-effect relationship undeniably
clear. Between the Duchess's secret marriage and her death, at
least four years elapse. Between Julia's secret arrangement with
Bosola and her death, barely four minutes pass. In short, not
only has Webster presented us with a parodic analogy of the
earlier wooing scene, he has provided us with a parodic minia-
ture tragedy here.

Even Julia's death is a diminished version of the Duchess's
death. She, too, dies stoically, without whining, revealing a
sense that she has received justice:

> I forgive you—
> This equal piece of justice you have done,
> For I betray'd your counsel to that fellow: . . .

'Tis weakness,
Too much to think what should have been done—I go
I know not whither.

(5. 2. 281–89)

Unlike the Duchess, Julia dies uncertain of her destination. The
Duchess hoped that she merited heaven on the basis of her
suffering; but just as the cruelty of her death and the dignity
of her dying do not redeem Julia, neither do they absolve the
Duchess of her responsibility for the condition of her world.
With relentless rhetorical consistency, Webster has Julia poisoned. Recall of his opening trope is no more gratuitous here
than elsewhere: Even Julia's death can be traced back to the
Duchess's initial action; it is for prying out the secret of his
complicity in the Duchess's death that the Cardinal poisons
Julia. That, it seems to me, is the point of Webster's parodic
wooing scene. By presenting this stark parody of the earlier
wooing scene after the Duchess's death, in the midst of all the
culminating horrors resulting from her action in that earlier
scene, and by analogically insisting upon and reducing the
Duchess's motivations in Julia's, Webster creates a strong coun-
terbalance to the sympathy engendered for her in Act 4, to any
sense that there has been no justice in her fate. The effect of
performance would underline this because the last time we see
both women, they are carried away from their "executions" in
Bosola's arms.[21]

21. Compare Lois Potter, "Realism Versus Nightmare: Problems of Staging
The Duchess of Malfi," p. 178.

6

Most Hard and Grievous Judgment

As I said in the last chapter, those who see the final act of *The Duchess of Malfi* as a kind of flawed addendum to an already completed action apparently have not perceived the complexity and coherence of the play's rhetoric. For his rhetorical purposes, Webster has made us value the Duchess, feel sympathy with her and pity and fear for her. Now, if that rhetoric is to be fully effective, he needs to get her off stage in order to bring his audience to full awareness of the consequences of actions with which they have been sympathetic.

Repeatedly, in discussing other aspects of the play, I have noted the ways in which Webster establishes its values for the audience and how he has sown, in imagery, characterization, and the shape of action the seeds of ironic and negative comment upon the Duchess. Yet, as we have seen, at the same time he adopts all sorts of strategies that guarantee that we will not condemn her and that we will be won to admire her. In other words, he seems to be hedging his bets, distancing himself while inviting the audience to implicate itself. He often gives the play's voice to characters whose personal quality is so questionable that the audience is almost certain to judge the utterance on the basis of that quality, not on its validity. The ironic metaphorical webs he spins are often so intricate that we are aware, for example, only of the wistful gentleness of the Duchess's animal imagery, not necessarily of its implications in the whole design. He makes the Duchess loved and admired by characters whom we approve, and he juxtaposes her charming domesticity with the rapacious politicality of her brothers. In a play in which most of the male characters are tyrants, cynics, flatterers, or toadies, and the only other women are a maid, a "strumpet," and a painted old woman, the Duchess can hardly avoid seeming a paragon of beauty, dignity, and wronged innocence. And we have but to read the critics to see how effective Webster's tactics have been. Perhaps they have been too effective for the play's own good.

As I have noted before, the persistence of the myth of the Duchess implies that again and again criticism of the play has suffered because critics have been overwhelmed by the Duchess's personality. Even one so rigorous in his judgment as Lagarde can say that it is because she is so magnificently woman at the end that all her faults are floated on a tide of pity and admiration.[1] Critics have assumed that this character sympathetically created by Webster was necessarily approved by Webster. That is to miss the point not only of the play but of the rhetoric characteristic of the genre; that is to assume that in depicting the effect of evil upon the human community Webster must depict all of his major characters simply, in terms of absolutes. In other words, because the Duchess seems to be a good, if fallible, individual, Webster must necessarily be condoning and approving of her across the board.

Certainly, on one level, the Duchess is good. We can sympathize with her longing for a quiet, love-filled domestic life; as Boklund has noted, approvingly, most often when we see the Duchess, she is engaged in some charmingly feminine domestic business. And that is the heart of the tragedy. She is not a private person. We may approve all that goes toward making her absolutely lovable on that level only if we, as she, forget what she is supposed to be. That is what I meant when I said in Chapter 1 that Webster's "ambivalence" consists in his capacity for judging her on more than one basis and allowing the play's rhetoric to imply which of these bases has greater communal value. It is the disparity between what she is and what she ought to be that creates the tragic dimension of this play, and it is that which Webster must make us feel if the play is to be rhetorically effective. We must have sympathy for her and realize how strong is the pull of her private desires if we are to feel how fragile is our security as human beings in a human community.[2]

The imagery and diction of the play repeatedly insist upon mortality, death, decay, and corruption. The cosmic uncertainty that infects man's thinking trembles across the play's linguistic surface. Bosola is its most consistent mouthpiece, but it shakes almost every character at one point or another. Life is an "ague"; "Heaven fashioned us of nothing, and we strive to become nothing"; "we cannot be suffered to do good when we've a mind to it." Man is caught and held or sent spinning

---

1. Fernand Lagarde, *John Webster,* p. 857.
2. See Robert Freeman Whitman, *Beyond Melancholy: John Webster and the Tragedy of Darkness,* ed. James Hogg, pp. 204–5.

on fortune's wheel. He is nothing but a box of worm seed. In the face of such insecurity men have fashioned moral and ethical systems, institutions, traditions, and conventions that may, at least, give this life some order and some certainty. Yet, as I said in Chapter 2, potential in each individual is a rebellion against those forms that are man's communal safeguards against chaos.

As we have seen, Antonio's opening speech pointed to the responsibility of the ruler for the health and order of the kingdom in that image of the prince's court as a common fountain from whence should flow pure silver drops in general. His image was prompted by his admiration for the French king who sought to "reduce both state and people to a *fixed order*" [my emphasis]. In short, in the value system of commonweal tragedy assumed by this speech and incorporated in the play, the ultimate earthly responsibility for maintaining the order so precious to the human community belongs, as I said, to the ruler. In the first three acts, we watch the Duchess circumvent, overturn, or pervert one after another of the norms, traditions, conventions, and institutions that are intended to insure that order. That she remains not only understandable but sympathetic to us while she is doing so gives us rather graphically the measure of our own potential for disruption and disorder.

It is mortally hard for men to abnegate the self in the interest of community, but this play demonstrates what happens when men, particularly rulers, are not willing to pay the price of that abnegation. Its ability to do this makes apparent the great rhetorical and didactic advantage that commonweal tragedy has over the political moralities in having as its ground the representation of the phenomenal world. The spectator of the morality play may simply fail to be convinced that his own state coincides with that of the mankind figure and may, therefore, feel unthreatened by that character's fate. But in watching *The Duchess of Malfi*, it is impossible not to feel fear that the rampant individuality in others that seeks only its own "good" may bring the structure of our world down around our ears and not to see that, then, the wolf in man will devour the bird. For its original audience, faced with abundant evidence of the verisimilitude of the play's perceptions, the old doctrines informing its generic features and its rhetorical perspective must have seemed doubly precious for being so negatively illustrated.

The fear of this individualism deepens when we are made to

realize that the individual's potential for unleashing evil and destroying order is not matched by an equal, individual, potential for countering evil and creating order. This, as I mentioned above, is brought out beautifully in *King Lear* when Cornwall's servant attempts to make his individual sword the instrument of justice—only to be run through from behind by Regan. In *The Duchess of Malfi*, Bosola's attempt to become the instrument of justice, once justice is no longer wedded to law, has a similar outcome and makes a similar point.

Bosola spends most of the play trying to get justice. At least that's how he defines his belief that princes should reward him for services rendered. What Bosola doesn't realize is that in rendering extra or illegal services to the Cardinal (murder) and Ferdinand (spying, torture, and murder), he has undercut the bases that define justice. When Ferdinand refuses to pay him after he has "executed" the Duchess, their exchange points this out:[3]

Bos.	I challenge
	The reward due to my service.
Ferd.	I'll tell thee,
	What I'll give thee—
Bos.	Do:—
Ferd.	I'll give thee a pardon
	For this murder:—
Bos.	Hah?
Ferd.	Yes: and 'tis
	The largest bounty I can study to do thee.
	By what authority didst thou execute
	This bloody sentence?
Bos.	By yours—
Ferd.	Mine? was I her judge?
	Did any ceremonial form of law
	Doom her to not-being? did a complete jury
	Deliver her conviction up i'th' court?
	Where shalt thou find the judgement register'd
	Unless in hell? See: like a bloody fool
	Th' hast forfeited thy life, and thou shalt die for't.
Bos.	The office of justice is perverted quite
	When one thief hangs another.

(4. 2. 293–307)

3. Ralph Berry's discussion of this scene in *The Art of John Webster,* pp. 123–25, as the "anagnorisis of the play," is excellent; but his final conclusion that, for Webster, there is a law of retribution that damns them both and that under that law Bosola does accomplish Justice, I cannot agree with.

Given the generic assumptions of commonweal tragedy, justice is most dangerously perverted when a ruler puts aside the law or takes the law into his own hands in order to satisfy personal desires; and this, of course, is what Ferdinand, the Cardinal, and the Duchess have done. The "ceremonial form of law" stands in relation to the spirit of justice as the outward form of a sacrament stands to the grace that validates it. In the case of law, "the ceremonial form"—the public performance and enforcement of rules through prescribed "rituals"—testifies to government and governed alike that both are upholding the bond that enables community. By surrendering to government the "right" to make and enforce his own rules, to impose his own absolutes, and to act according to his own needs and desires regardless of those of other men, a man makes himself vulnerable to the government and to those other men, unless he can assume that they, too, will honor the ceremonial forms of law that, then, enable all to live together in justice and peace.

From the standpoint of law, as I have implicitly defined it here, is Ferdinand's ritualized murder of the Duchess any less "legal" than her private marriage rites with Antonio? Ferdinand himself denies its legality, but that denial reflects the play's judgment upon her private rites as well, implying again, as I argued in Chapter 5, the condign nature of her punishment. In both cases there is no public "ceremonial form of law." Once again we see illustrated that truism of commonweal tragedy that when such law and power are separated, the possibility for justice evaporates. The will that wields the strongest and most cunning sword then becomes the law, and that is not the establishment of justice and order, only of the possibility for infinite conflict. As Ulysses puts it in that oft-quoted speech from *Troilus and Cressida:*

> Force should be right; or rather, right and wrong,
> Between whose endless jar justice resides,
> Should lose their names, and so should justice too.
> Then everything includes itself in power,
> Power into will, will into appetite;
> And appetite, an universal wolf,
> So doubly seconded with will and power,
> Must make perforce an universal prey,
> And last eat up himself.
>
> (1. 3. 114–24)

When Bosola, goaded by Ferdinand's treachery, goes to Rome, his motive is revenge. Yet, when he pretends to enter into the Cardinal's plot to kill Antonio, he thinks he sees the possibility for becoming an instrument of justice. That he then unwittingly kills Antonio is the play's ironic comment on the efficacy—nay, the very possibility—of individual justice.[4]

Critics have complained about the bit of mistaken identity that foils Bosola's intentions, about the contrivedness of the Cardinal's trick to keep the courtiers away that results in his death, and about the melodrama of Ferdinand's mistakenly wounding his brother. In short, they have seen in the last act a sort of dramatic chaos upon which Webster has imposed a specious order. There is no question of the frenetic quality of the last scene. Yet, as I said earlier, Webster's problem is that he must depict the force of disorder the Duchess has loosed. What we have in this act is Webster's attempt to present evil in a final paroxysm of self-consumption. We could hardly expect that to be presented as an orderly process. As a matter of fact, the last scene seems to me a perfect representation of Ulysses' prediction—especially in light of his use of the wolf image of disorder that is reified in Ferdinand's lycanthropy.

Thus, the play bears out the dangers of unchecked individualism, and the almost universal critical admiration felt for the Duchess when she speaks her famous line—"I am Duchess of Malfi still"—attests to the degree to which that radical individualism is potential in all of us. For a Renaissance audience the awe and aura of noble rank might have momentarily enabled an ambivalent response; yet, never in the play has the Duchess acted as duchess, acted as a ruler without self-interest. Her every action has been dictated by her desires and needs as a woman and a private person, not by her duties and responsibilities as a ruler. That line points to her self-delusion about the nature of greatness and to her lack of integrity as a ruler. On that level the Duchess comes to no tragic awareness.

4. This question of "individual justice" and its speciousness because based on arbitrary use of discretion and power may explain Edgar's elaborate ritual of challenging Edmund in *Lear*. It seems inorganic to the play; yet, because the institution of justice has been subverted and to appeal to Albany who has been connected with the forces of injustice would implicitly recognize him as "law," Edgar resorts to forms, to ceremony, to confer an aspect of communal justice on his action and remove from it any taint of vengeance, for example personal "justice."

Taken in the full context of her holding court over a group of madmen and of her exchange with Bosola, in which she has questioned her identity and been progressively undercut by his comments, her line sounds more like hysterical assertion than certain affirmation of identity. And Bosola counters that assertion as quickly and bluntly as he had her others. The very rhythm of these speeches argues against Webster's having intended it as a great moment of self-affirmation. Since the Duchess has never in this play behaved like a duchess, her line has the very specious sound of a continuing solipsism. To see it as so many have, as a moment in which she makes us proud of our individuality, is to convict oneself in terms of the values of the play. To say, as Berry does, that "Duchesshood" consists, finally, in realizing her identity by dying like a duchess, behaving herself at the last as a duchess should,[5] is, I think, to ignore the fact that Julia dies with the same dignity and courage.

The generic expectations of commonweal tragedy would not lead an audience who shared those expectations to believe that the Duchess's private virtues and private sufferings excused her from judgment as a prince. The orthodox political doctrine that points to the stark justice of her treatment (by the play, if not by Ferdinand) is voiced by Elyot: "For moste harde and greuous iugement shall be on them that haue rule ouer other. To the poure man mercy is graunted, but the great man shall sufre great tourments."[6]

In terms of the world of the play, and the genre's set on that world, there is a terrible, ironic justice at work here. As I said earlier, when the Duchess turned her back on public responsibility to satisfy her private desires, she created the conditions in which power and justice would be separated. Ferdinand's treatment of her is, of course, monstrous, yet, as I attempted to show in Chapter 5, given her exemplary role, some punishment is demanded. Expressing the political norms assumed by commonweal tragedy, James had said, "the people that see you not within, can not judge of you but according to the out-ward appearance of your action and companie, which only is subject to their sight."[7] In the sight of the people, the Duchess is still a strumpet; her "noble lie" and banishment of Antonio as a dishonest steward, her flight, and her loss of the duchy can only

5. Ralph Berry, *The Art of John Webster*, p. 147.
6. Sir Elyot, *The Book of the Governour*, p. 118.
7. James I, *Basilikon Doron*, p. 77.

have confirmed them in this opinion. Should the Duchess live happily-ever-after, their belief in justice would be radically shaken.

Shakespeare gives dramatic voice to this question in *King Lear*. The comments of the two servants about Cornwall and Regan after the blinding of Gloucester and the killing of the servant who attempted to stop it reflect the assumption of commonweal tragedy that in the relationship between a ruler's action and his fate, the people must see an example of, and become convinced that there is, a principle of justice operative in the universe:

> *2 Servant:* I'll never care what wickedness I do,
>   If this man come to good.
> *3 Servant:*   If she live long
>   And in the end meet the old course of death,
>   Women will all turn monsters.
>
>   (3. 7. 99–102)

Appalling as it seems, from the standpoint of those she ruled, the Duchess has, at last, provided an example that conduces to the common weal, an exemplary lesson of the consequences of radical individualism.

Apparently, we have lost certain assumptions about the relative value of communality and individuality that would render us as capable as Jacobeans of immediately recognizing how firmly the play rejects an individualism that places itself above communal responsibility.[8] In the last act Webster makes that condemnation clear. Unless we realize this, Delio's final lines make no sense:

>   These wretched eminent things
> Leave no more fame behind 'em than should one
> Fall in a frost, and leave his print in snow;
> As soon as the sun shines, it ever melts,
> Both form, and matter:—I have ever thought
> Nature doth nothing so great, for great men,
> As when she's pleas'd to make them lords of truth:
> *Integrity of life is fame's best friend,*
> *Which nobly, beyond death, shall crown the end.*
>
>   (5. 5. 113–21)

8. See Clifford Leech, *John Webster: A Critical Study,* p. 77. In discussing her line and its implications, Leech compares it to Flamineo's death speech in *The White Devil* and then says, "there is a grandeur in the egotism but its implications are essentially anarchic."

Integrity of life is to seem what you are and to be what you ought to be, according to your beliefs, station, duties, and responsibilities. It is implicitly defined in the "character" of "A Reverend Judge" attributed to Webster: "His care is to appeare such to the people, as he would have them be; and to bee himself such as he appeares: for vertue cannot seem one thing, and be another."[9] The Duchess was often not what she seemed and never, in the action of the play, what she should have been according to her station and its responsibilities to the human community. Like those other "wretched eminent things"—her brothers—she failed utterly to achieve integrity of life. Worse, in their duplicity, willfulness, and radical individualism, all three of these princes have offered to those they ruled an example "curs'd" in its nihilistic implications. Bosola voices the desperation of those faced with no other example: "I will not imitate things glorious, / No more than base: I'll be mine own example" (5. 4. 81–82). The ensuing action insists with violent immediacy on the consequences of this desperate "choice."

As Delio said: "They pass through whirlpools and deep woes do shun, / Who the event weigh, ere the action's done." Because of the complexity of Webster's rhetoric, the Duchess may escape the whirlpool of censure and shun the woe of condemnation through most of the action, but the events do weigh her before the action's done. Judged against her own claim that she can live and die like a prince, she is found wanting. She failed to understand, much less achieve, the integrity of life that would have made "I am Duchess of Malfi still" an earned and saving affirmation. This essential failure makes the play a commonweal tragedy.

9. "A Reverend Judge," *The Complete Works of John Webster,* vol. 4, ed. F. L. Lucas, p. 38.

Appendix

A vertuous Widdow

Is the Palme-tree, that thrives not after the supplanting of her husband. For her Childrens sake she first marries, for she married that she might have children, and for their sakes she marries no more. She is like the purest gold, only imploid for Princes meddals, she never receives but one mans impression; the large jointure moves her not, titles of honor cannot sway her. To change her name were, shee thinkes, to commit a sin should make her asham'd of her husbands Calling: shee thinkes shee hath traveld all the world in one man; the rest of her time therefore shee directs to heaven. Her maine superstition is, shee thinkes her husbands ghost would walke should shee not performe his Will: shee would doe it, were there no Prerogative Court. Shee gives much to pious uses, without any hope to merit by them: and as one Diamond fashions another; so is shee wrought into workes of Charity, with the dust or ashes of her husband. Shee lives to see her selfe full of time: being so necessary for earth, God calles her not to heaven, till she bee very aged: and even then, though her naturall strength faile her, shee stands like an ancient *Piramid;* which the lesse it growes to mans eye, the nearer it reaches to heaven: this latter Chastity of Hers, is more grave and reverend, then that ere shee was married; for in it is neither hope, nor longing, nor feare, nor jealousie. Shee ought to bee a mirrour for our yongest Dames, to dresse themselves by, when shee is fullest of wrinkles. No calamity can now come neere her, for in suffering the losse of her husband, shee accounts all the rest trifles: she hath laid his dead body in the worthyest monument that can be: Shee hath buried it in her owne heart. To conclude, shee is a Relique, that without any supers[ti]tion in the world, though she will not be kist, yet may be reverenc't.

[*The Complete Works of John Webster,* vol. 4, ed. F. L. Lucas (New York: Hill and Wang, 1966), pp. 38–39.]

Bibliography

Primary Works

James I, King of Great Britain. *Basilikon Doron,* 1599. Menston, England: The Scolar Press Ltd., 1969.

Painter, William. *The Palace of Pleasure.* Vol. 3. Edited by Joseph Jacobs. Hildesheim: Georg Olms Verlagsbuch, 1890.

Schell, Edgar T. and Shuchter, J. D., eds. *English Morality Plays and Moral Interludes.* New York: Holt, Rinehart and Winston, 1969.

The Complete Plays and Poems of William Shakespeare. Edited by William Allan Neilson and Charles Jarvis Hill. Cambridge: Houghton Mifflin, 1942.

Symonds, John, ed. *John Webster and Cyril Tourneur: Four Plays.* New York: Hill and Wang, 1966.

The Complete Works of John Webster. 4 vols. Edited by F. L. Lucas. New York: Gordian Press, 1966.

Webster, John. *The Duchess of Malfi.* Edited by Elizabeth Brennan. New York: Hill and Wang, 1966.

_____. *The Duchess of Malfi.* Edited by John Russell Brown. Cambridge, Mass.: Harvard University Press, 1964.

_____. *The Duchess of Malfi.* Edited by Clive Hart. Edinburgh: Oliver and Boyd, 1972.

Critical, Political, and Historical Studies

Adams, Henry Hitch. *English Domestic or Homiletic Tragedy.* New York: Columbia University Press, 1965.

Akrigg, G. P. V. *Jacobean Pageant or the Court of King James I.* Cambridge, Mass.: Harvard University Press, 1963.

Allison, Alexander. "Ethical Themes in *The Duchess of Malfi.*" *Studies in English Literature* 4 (1964):263–73.

Ansari, K. H. *John Webster: Image Patterns and Canon.* Delhi, 1969.

Archer, William. "The Duchess of Malfi." *Nineteenth Century* 87 (1920):126–32.

Auerbach, Erich. *Mimesis: The Representation of Reality in Western Literature.* Princeton: Princeton University Press, 1953.

Baker, Howard. *Induction to Tragedy.* Baton Rouge: Louisiana State University Press, 1939.

Berlin, Normand. "*The Duchess of Malfi:* Act V and Genre." *Genre* 3 (1970):351–63.

Berry, Ralph. *The Art of John Webster.* Oxford: Clarendon Press, 1972.

Bevington, David. *From MANKIND to Marlowe: Growth of Structure in the Popular Drama of Tudor England.* Cambridge, Mass.: Harvard University Press, 1962.

_____. *Tudor Drama and Politics: A Critical Approach to Topical Meaning.* Cambridge, Mass.: Harvard University Press, 1968.

Bodtke, Richard A. *Tragedy and the Jacobean Temper: The Major Plays of John Webster.* Jacobean Drama Studies 2, edited by James Hogg. Salzburg: Institut für Englische Sprache und Literatur, 1972.

Bogard, Travis. *The Tragic Satire of John Webster.* Berkeley: University of California Press, 1955.

Boklund, Gunnar. *The Duchess of Malfi: Sources, Themes, Characters.* Cambridge, Mass.: Harvard University Press, 1962.

Booth, Wayne C. *A Rhetoric of Irony.* Chicago: University of Chicago Press, 1974.

Bradbrook, M. C. *English Dramatic Form: A History of Its Development.* New York: Barnes & Noble, 1965.

_____. *Themes and Conventions of Elizabethan Tragedy.* Cambridge: Cambridge University Press, 1935.

_____. "Two Notes Upon Webster." *Modern Language Review* 42 (1947):281–91.

Bradford, Gamaliel. "The Women of Middleton and Webster." *Sewanee Review* 29 (1921):14–29.

Brennan, Elizabeth. "The Relationship Between Brother and Sister in the Plays of John Webster." *Modern Language Review* 18 (1963):488–94.

Brodwin, Leonora Leet. *Elizabethan Love Tragedy, 1587–1625.* New York: New York University Press, 1971.

Brooke, Rupert. *John Webster and the Elizabethan Drama.* New York: John Lane, 1916.

Brysson-Morrison, N. *Mary Queen of Scots.* New York: The Vanguard Press, 1974.

Calderwood, James L. "*The Duchess of Malfi:* Styles of Ceremony." *Essays in Criticism* 2 (1962):133–47.

Camden, Carroll. *The Elizabethan Woman.* Houston: Elsevier Press, 1952.

Camoin, François André. *The Revence [sic] Convention in Tourneur, Webster and Middleton.* Jacobean Drama Studies 20, edited by

James Hogg. Salzburg: Institut für Englische Sprache und Literatur, 1973.

Campbell, O. J. "The Salvation of King Lear." *The Journal of English Literary History* 15 (1948):93–109.

Champion, Larry S. "Webster's *The White Devil* and Jacobean Tragic Perspective." *Texas Studies in Language and Literature* 16 (Fall 1974):447–62.

Colie, Rosalie. *The Resources of Kind: Genre Theory in the Renaissance.* Berkeley: University of California Press, 1973.

Cook, David. "The Extreme Situation: A Study of Webster's Tragedies." *KOMOS* 2 (1969):9–15.

Craig, Hardin. "Morality Plays and Elizabethan Drama." *Shakespeare Quarterly* 1 (1950):64–72.

Cunliffe, John W. *The Influence of Seneca on Elizabethan Tragedy.* London: Macmillan, 1893.

Cushman, L. W. *The Devil and the Vice in the English Dramatic Literature Before Shakespeare.* Halle: M. Niemeyer, 1910.

Davies, Cecil W. "The Structure of *The Duchess of Malfi:* An Approach." *English* 12 (1958):89–93.

Davison, M. H. Armstrong. *The Casket Letters: Solution to the Mystery of Mary Queen of Scots and the Murder of Lord Darnley.* Washington, D. C.: The University Press, 1965.

Davison, Richard Allan. "John Webster's Moral View Reexamined." *Moderna Sprak* 63 (1969):213–23.

Dent, R. W. *John Webster's Borrowings.* Berkeley: University of California Press, 1960.

Donaldson, Gordon. *Mary Queen of Scots.* London: English Universities Press, 1974.

Driscoll, James P. "Integrity of Life in *The Duchess of Malfi.*" *Drama Survey* 6 (1967):42–53.

Dwyer, William W. *A Study of Webster's Use of Renaissance Natural and Moral Philosophy.* Jacobean Drama Studies 18, edited by James Hogg. Salzburg: Institut für Englische Sprache und Literatur, 1972.

Einstein, Lewis. *Tudor Ideals.* New York: Russell & Russell, 1962.

Ekeblad, Inga-stina. "The 'Impure Art' of John Webster." *Review of English Studies,* n.s. 9 (1958):253–67.

Ellis-Fermor, Una. *The Jacobean Drama.* London: Methuen, 1961.

Elyot, Sir Thomas. *The Book of the Governour.* New York: Dutton & Company, 1907.

Farnham, Willard. *The Medieval Heritage of Elizabethan Tragedy.*

Berkeley: University of California Press, 1936.

Fenton, Geoffrey. *A Form of Christian Pollicie, 1574.* The English Experience, No. 454. Amsterdam: Theatrvm Orbis Terrarvm, Ltd., 1972.

Forker, Charles R. "Love, Death, and Fame: The Grotesque Tragedy of John Webster." *Anglia* 91 (1972):194–218.

Fraser, Antonia. *Mary Queen of Scots.* London: Weidenfeld & Nicolson, 1969.

Gallagher, Ligeia, ed., *More's UTOPIA and its Critics.* Chicago: Scott, Foresman, 1964.

Gianetti, Louis D. "A Contemporary View of *The Duchess of Malfi.*"*Comparative Drama* 3 (1969–1970):297–307.

Goreau, Eloise K. *Integrity of Life: Allegorical Imagery in the Plays of John Webster.* Jacobean Drama Studies 32, edited by James Hogg. Salzburg: Institut für Englische Sprache und Literatur, 1972.

Griffin, Robert P. *John Webster: Politics and Tragedy.* Jacobean Drama Studies 12, edited by James Hogg. Salzburg: Institut für Englische Sprache und Literatur, 1972.

Gunby, D. C. "*The Duchess of Malfi:* A Theological Approach." *John Webster: Proceedings of the York Symposium, 2d, Langwith College, 1969,* edited by Brian Morris, pp. 181–204. London: Ernest Benson Ltd., 1970.

Harrison, G. B. *A Second Jacobean Journal: Being a Record of Those Things Most Talked of during the Years 1607 to 1610.* Ann Arbor: University of Michigan Press, 1958.

Haworth, Peter. *English Hymns and Ballads and Other Studies in Popular Literature.* Philadelphia: The Folcroft Press, Inc., 1969.

Henke, James T. "John Webster's Motif of 'Consuming': An Approach to the Dramatic Unity of *The White Devil* and *The Duchess of Malfi.*" *Neuphilologische Mitteilungen* 76 (1975):625–41.

Hirsch, E. D., Jr. *Validity in Interpretation.* New Haven: Yale University Press, 1967.

Jack, Ian. "The Case of John Webster." *Scrutiny* 16 (1949):38–43.

Jorgensen, Paul. *Our Naked Frailties.* Berkeley: University of California Press, 1971.

Kantorowicz, Ernest. *The King's Two Bodies.* Princeton: Princeton University Press, 1957.

Kirsch, Arthur C. *Jacobean Dramatic Perspectives.* Charlottesville: The University Press of Virginia, 1972.

Kitto, H. D. F. *Form and Meaning in Drama.* London: Methuen, 1960.

Knight, G. Wilson. "The Duchess of Malfi." *Malahat Review* 4 (1967):90–91.

Krieger, Murray. *A Window to Criticism*. Princeton: Princeton University Press, 1964.

Lagarde, Fernand. *John Webster*. 2 vols. Association Des Publications de la Faculté Des Lettres Et Sciences Humaines de Toulouse, 1968.

Lee, Maurice, Jr. *James Stewart, Earl of Moray: A Political Study of the Reformation in Scotland*. New York: Columbia University Press, 1953.

Leech, Clifford. "An Addendum to Webster's Duchess." *Philological Quarterly* 25 (1958):253–56.

_____. *John Webster: A Critical Study*. London: The Hogarth Press, 1951.

_____. *The Duchess of Malfi*. London: Edward Arnold, 1963.

_____. "The Function of Locality in the Plays of Shakespeare and his Contemporaries." In *The Elizabethan Theatre*, edited by David R. Galloway, pp. 103–16. London: Macmillan, 1969.

Lever, John W. *The Tragedy of State*. London: Methuen, 1971.

Levin, Richard. *The Multiple Plot in English Renaissance Drama*. Chicago: University of Chicago Press, 1971.

Luisi, David. "The Function of Bosola in *The Duchess of Malfi*." *English Studies* 53 (1972):509–13.

Mack, Maynard. *Killing the King: Three Studies in Shakespeare's Tragic Structure*. New Haven: Yale University Press, 1973.

MacKisack, May. *The Fourteenth Century: 1307–1399*. Oxford: Clarendon Press, 1959.

Mahaney, William E. *Deception in the John Webster Plays: An Analytical Study*. Jacobean Drama Studies 9, edited by James Hogg. Salzburg: Institut für Englische Sprache und Literatur, 1972.

Manheim, Michael. *The Weak King Dilemma in the Shakespearean History Play*. Syracuse: Syracuse University Press, 1973.

Moore, Don D. *John Webster and His Critics, 1617–1964*. Baton Rouge: Louisiana State University Press, 1966.

Mulryne, J. R. "Webster and the Uses of Tragicomedy." In *John Webster: Proceedings of the York Symposium, 2d, Langwith College, 1969*, edited by Brian Morris, pp. 137–38. London: Ernest Benson, 1970.

_____. "*The White Devil* and *The Duchess of Malfi*." *Jacobean Theatre*. Stratford-Upon-Avon Studies, No. 1., edited by John Russell

Brown and Bernard Harris, pp. 201–26. New York: St. Martin's Press.

Mumby, Frank Arthur. *The Fall of Mary Stuart: A Narrative in Contemporary Letters.* London: Constable and Company, 1921.

Murray, Peter. *A Study of John Webster.* The Hague: Mouton, 1969.

Owst, G. R. *Literature and Pulpit in Medieval England.* New York: Barnes and Noble, 1961.

Ornstein, Robert. *A Kingdom for a Stage: The Achievement of Shakespeare's History Plays.* Cambridge, Mass.: Harvard University Press, 1972.

————. *The Moral Vision of Jacobean Tragedy.* Madison, Wisconsin: University of Wisconsin Press, 1960.

Partridge, Eric. *Shakespeare's Bawdy.* New York: E. P. Dutton, 1969.

Peterson, Joyce E. "The Paradox of Disintegrating Form in *Mundus et Infans.*" *English Literary Renaissance* 7 (Winter 1977):3–16.

Phillips, James Emerson. *Images of a Queen: Mary Stuart in Sixteenth Century Literature.* Berkeley: University of California Press, 1964.

Potter, Lois. "Realism Versus Nightmare: Problems of Staging *The Duchess of Malfi.*" In *The Triple Bond: Plays, Mainly Shakespearean, in Performance,* edited by Joseph G. Price, pp. 170–89. University Park: Pennsylvania State University Press, 1975.

Price, Hereward T. "The Function of Imagery in Webster." *Publications of the Modern Language Association* 70 (1955):717–39.

Reese, M. M. *The Tudors and Stuarts.* London: Edward Arnold, 1940.

Ribner, Irving. *The English History Play in the Age of Shakespeare.* Princeton: Princeton University Press, 1957.

————. *Jacobean Tragedy: The Quest for Moral Order.* London: Methuen, 1962.

————. "The Morality Roots of the Tudor History Plays." *Tulane Studies in English* 4 (1954):21–43.

————. *Patterns in Shakespearean Tragedy.* London: Methuen, 1960.

Righter, Anne. *Shakespeare and the Idea of the Play.* London: Chatto & Windus, 1962.

Rossiter, A. P. *English Drama From Early Times to the Elizabethans.* London: Hutchinson's University Library, 1950.

Salingar, L. G. "*The Revenger's Tragedy* and the Morality Tradition." *Scrutiny* 6 (1938):402–24.

Schell, Edgar T. "Who Said That—Hamlet or *Hamlet?*" *Shakespeare Quarterly* 24 (1972):135–46.

Schuman, Samuel. "The Ring and the Jewel in Webster's Trage-
dies." *Texas Studies in Literature and Language* 14 (1972):253–68.
Scott-Kilvert, Ian. *John Webster.* London: Longmans, Green,
1964.
Seiden, Melvin. *The Revenge Tragedy in Websterian Tragedy.* Jaco-
bean Drama Studies 15, edited by James Hogg. Salzburg:
Institut für Englische Sprache und Literatur, 1972.
Sharpe, Robert B. *Irony in the Drama.* Chapel Hill: University of
North Carolina, 1959.
Shaw, Sharon K. "Medea on Pegasus: Some Speculations on the
Parallel Rise of Women and Melodrama and the Jacobean
Stage." *Ball State University Forum* 14 (1972):13–21.
Spivack, Bernard. *Shakespeare and the Allegory of Evil.* New York:
Columbia University Press, 1958.
Sternlicht, Sanford. *John Webster's Imagery and the Webster Canon.*
Jacobean Drama Studies 1, edited by James Hogg. Salzburg:
Institut für Englische Sprache und Literatur, 1972.
Stilling, Roger. *Love and Death in Renaissance Tragedy.* Baton Rouge:
Louisiana State University Press, 1976.
Stoll, Elmer. *John Webster: The Periods of His Work as Determined by
His Relation to the Drama of His Day.* Boston: A. Mudge, 1905.
Strickland, Agnes. *The Life of Mary Queen of Scots.* 2 vols. London:
George Bell and Sons, 1873.
Sullivan, S. W. "The Tendency to Rationalize in *The White Devil*
and *The Duchess of Malfi.*" *Yearbook of English Studies* 4 (1974):
77–84.
Thomson, George Malcolm. *The Crime of Mary Stuart.* New York:
E. P. Dutton & Company, 1967.
Tillyard, E. M. W. *The Elizabethan World Picture.* London: Chatto
& Windus, 1958.
_____. *Shakespeare's History Plays.* London: Chatto & Windus,
1961.
Tomlinson, T. B. *A Study of Elizabethan and Jacobean Tragedy.* Lon-
don: Cambridge University Press, 1964.
Vernon, P. F. "The Duchess of Malfi's Guilt." *Notes & Queries* 10
(1963):335–38.
Wadsworth, Frank W. "Webster's *Duchess of Malfi* in the Light
of Some Contemporary Ideas on Marriage and Remarriage."
Philological Quarterly 25 (1956):394–407.
Wang, Tso-Liang. *The Literary Reputation of John Webster to 1830.*
Jacobean Drama Studies 59, edited by James Hogg. Salzburg:
Institut für Englische Sprache und Literatur, 1974.

West, Muriel. *The Devil and John Webster.* Jacobean Drama Studies
    11, edited by James Hogg. Salzburg: Institut für Englische
    Sprache und Literatur, 1974.

Whitman, Robert Freeman. *Beyond Melancholy: John Webster and the
    Tragedy of Darkness.* Jacobean Drama Studies 4, edited by James
    Hogg. Salzburg: Institut für Englische Sprache und Literatur,
    1973.

———. "The Moral Paradox of Webster's Tragedy." *PMLA* 90
    (October 1975):894–903.

Williams, Arnold. *The Drama of Medieval England.* East Lansing:
    Michigan State University Press, 1961.

Wilson, J. Dover. *The Fortunes of Falstaff.* Cambridge, Eng.: The
    University Press, 1944.